Vorwort

Das vorliegende Buch *Business Situations* ist eine **Soforthilfe für den geschäftlichen Alltag**. In der Realität des geschäftlichen Alltags ist es nicht möglich, bei sprachlichen Problemen und Aufgaben auf umfassende Lehrwerke zurückzugreifen und die entsprechenden Kapitel nachzulesen. Dazu fehlt in der Regel die Zeit. Um gezielt und schnell Antworten zu erhalten, bedarf es eines benutzerfreundlichen und situationsangemessenen Zugriffs. Dieser Zugriff ist in der Soforthilfe gewährt.

Das **Inhaltsverzeichnis** verschafft einen Überblick über die Themen.

In der Soforthilfe werden typische **Sprachfunktionen** wie Entschuldigungen, Zustimmung, Danken und Ablehnung, **Situationen** wie Besprechungen und Verhandlungen, **Sprachtätigkeiten** wie Briefeschreiben, Verfassen von E-Mails oder Telefonieren und **Interaktions- sowie Konversationsstrategien** (Eröffnung und Beenden eines Gesprächs, Antworten, Unterbrechen, Variation in der Abfolge) behandelt. Sprachlich werden die Themen unterstützt durch

- nützliche Phrasen, Redewendungen und Dialoge,
- typische Beispiele und
- Tipps phonetischer, grammatischer, lexikalischer, stilistischer und soziokultureller Art.

Im **Extrateil** befinden sich

- die englische Aussprache von Buchstaben sowie die internationale Buchstabierliste,
- Hinweise zu Zahlen, Daten sowie Zeitangaben,
- ein Organigramm und
- zwei alphabetische Wortschatzlisten. Die **englisch-deutsche** Liste bezieht sich ausschließlich auf den vor-

liegenden Buchtext. Das **deutsch-englische** Vokabular enthält die im Buchtext erwähnten und darüber hinaus weitere nützliche Ausdrücke aus der Geschäftssprache.

Das übersichtliche **Layout** und das **Format** des Bandes tragen schließlich zur Benutzerfreundlichkeit bei.

FREMDSPRACHENTEXTE

Business Situations

Soforthilfe für den geschäftlichen Alltag

Von Margaret Nester
und Burkhard Dretzke

Philipp Reclam jun. Stuttgart

RECLAMS UNIVERSAL-BIBLIOTHEK Nr. 19727
Alle Rechte vorbehalten
Copyright © 2007 Philipp Reclam jun. GmbH & Co., Stuttgart
Umschlaggraphik: Eva Knoll, Stuttgart
Gesamtherstellung: Reclam, Ditzingen. Printed in Germany 2008
RECLAM, UNIVERSAL-BIBLIOTHEK und RECLAMS
UNIVERSAL-BIBLIOTHEK sind eingetragene Marken
der Philipp Reclam jun. GmbH & Co., Stuttgart
ISBN 978-3-15-019727-1

www.reclam.de

Contents

Meeting People

Social Situations

Business Communication

Extras (Appendix)

Meeting People

1. Introducing yourself

You may find you have to introduce yourself on many occasions, for example during a presentation, at a conference or simply when meeting someone for the first time. The following phrases should be helpful. You would of course begin by saying *Good morning* (until midday) / *Good afternoon* (until about 6 pm) / *Good evening* (after 6 pm), or even *Hello/Hi* on an informal occasion. You only say *Good night* before you go to bed.

Useful Phrases

May I introduce myself? I'm … / My name's …
I don't think we've met before. I'm …
I don't think we've been introduced. I'm …

Replying to an introduction

How do you do? And I'm …
Pleased to meet you. My name's …
Nice to meet you. I'm …

> **Conversation (1)**
> A: Good morning. I don't think we've met before. I'm Susan Roberts. I work for British Telecom.
> B: Pleased to meet you. I'm James Swinbourne. I'm with Hewlett Packard.

Conversation (2)

A: Hello. May I introduce myself? I'm Paul Simon.
B: Nice to meet you, Mr Simon. My name's Jane Barton.
A: Please call me Paul.
B: And I'm Jane.

Note

To get on first-name terms (allow someone to call you by your first name) you say *My name's Paul Simon. Please call me Paul.*

Conversation (3)

A: I don't think we've been introduced. I'm Fernando Velasquez.
B: Nice to meet you, but I'm sorry, I didn't quite catch your name.
A: It's Fernando Velasquez. Let me give you my card.

Note

If you did not understand someone's name, it is more polite to say *I'm sorry, I didn't catch your name* than *I didn't hear/understand your name.*

Describing your job

In a business context, it is always useful to be able to say a few words about your job or to comment on the occasion. The following phrases should help you to do this.

Question:

What do you do?

Possible answers:

I'm **an** engineer / **a** secretary / **a** sales rep etc.

I'm **in** marketing / the chemicals business/advertising. (i.e. business area).

I work **for** IBM.

Do you work **at** Siemens?

Are you **with** Microsoft?

I'm based **in** ... (country/city).

I work **in** the sales department. / I'm **in** sales.

I'm responsible **for** transport / **for** organis**ing** fairs and exhibitions.

I'm self-employed. I have my own business.

I work freelance. I'm a freelance writer/designer.

Conversation (4)

A: Hello. I don't think we've met. I'm Joe Anderson.

B: Hi. Nice to meet you. I'm Jake Newman.

A: What do you think of the conference? I'm in the construction business, so I'm finding it quite informative. What do you do?

B: Well, I'm a civil engineer, so I agree it's quite useful.

Tips

- It is normal to use contractions in conversations. (*I'm, it's, we're, she's, we've, I don't, he doesn't, they didn't* etc.)
- Using first names is very common in Anglo-American companies and business contexts.

- *How do you do* is not a real question. It means *Pleased/Nice to meet you.*
- In Anglo-American cultures, it is usual to shake hands only the first time you meet someone.
- The question *What do you do?* means *What job do you do?*
- You use an indefinite article when describing your job. *I'm **an** engineer. / She's **a** secretary.*
- Notice the prepositions you can use to talk about where you work. *I work **for** an engineering company. / Do you work **at** ICL? / I'm **with** Microsoft.*
- The abbreviations *e.g.* and *i.e.* mean *for example* and *that is* respectively.
- A verb used after a preposition is in the *-ing* form. *I'm responsible **for** organis**ing** fairs.*

2. Introducing Other People and Greetings at Subsequent Meetings

A. Introducing Other People

The following phrases are useful for introducing other people to one another.

May I introduce ...?   Do you know ...?
I'd like to introduce ...   Have you met ...?
I'd like you to meet ...   This is ...

Replying to an introduction

How do you do? / Pleased to meet you. / Nice to meet you.

Conversation (1)

(John introduces Adam Walker to Sophie Bennett)
John: Sophie, I'd like you to meet a colleague of mine, Adam Walker.
Sophie: Nice to meet you, Mr Walker.
Adam: Pleased to meet you, too. And please call me Adam.

Conversation (2)

(Jim introduces Dr Peter Klaus to his colleague, Paul Bradshaw)
Jim: Paul, have you met Dr Klaus?
Paul: I don't think so. How do you do?
Dr Klaus: Nice to meet you.

Conversation (3)

(Sarah introduces Tim to Marie Chauchix)

Sarah: Tim, this is Marie Chauchix from our Paris office. Marie, this is Tim Harper.

Marie: Hello, Tim. Nice to meet you.

Tim: Nice to meet you, too. I'm sorry, I didn't quite catch your name.

Marie: I know. A lot of people have problems with it. It's Marie Chauchix.

Conversation (4)

(Paul introduces Martin to Sue Ripley)

Paul: Sue, have you met Martin Bell? He's our sales manager.

Sue: No, I don't think so. How do you do?

Martin: Nice to meet you. Are you in sales, too?

Sue: No. I'm in human resources, actually. I work for IBM.

Tips

- A man uses the title *Mr*, whereas women may use the title *Mrs* or *Ms*. *Mrs* is used for a married woman; *Ms* is used for unmarried or married women to avoid the distinction in marital status. It is best to use the title preferred by the person herself. *Miss* for unmarried women is old-fashioned and very rarely used these days.
- These days, people usually introduce themselves and one another by using first and second names. *This is my colleague Bill Bryant* (unless the situation is very formal and you are introducing a person with a higher status). *This is Professor Bryant.*

- Academic titles are used as follows: *Doctor Mottram*; *Professor Smith*. These are used for men and women and regardless of other qualifications, e.g. **Professor Dr Smith* is incorrect.

B. Greetings at Subsequent Meetings

Introductory remarks to people you have already met can range from a simple *How are you?* to enquiries about the family, job or current project. The answers are normally positive or neutral, but may be negative. The question *How do you do?* is incorrect in this situation.

Hello / Hi / Good morning / Good afternoon / Good evening.
Nice to see you again.
How are you? / How is your wife? / And the children? / And the family?
How are things (with you)?
How's the project going/coming along?
How's your new colleague doing?

Introductory remark	Response
Nice to see you again.	Nice to see you, too.
How are you?	Very well. / Fine, thanks. And you?
	Not too bad, thanks. And you?
	Not too good, I'm afraid.
How are things (with you)?	Fine. / Okay, thanks.

How's the new project going?	Fine. / Not too good. / Well, ...
How's Jim Bradshaw doing?	Fine. / Not too bad. / Well, ...

Note

If someone answers *Not too good* in response to the enquiry *How are you?*, you would normally follow up with an additional enquiry like *Oh dear! What's wrong?* or *I'm sorry to hear that. What's the matter?* to show interest or sympathy.

Conversation (1) *(fairly informal)*

Susan: Hello, Paul. Nice to see you again. How are you?

Paul: Fine, thanks. And you?

Susan: Very well, thanks. So, how's the Loxton Project coming along?

Paul: Actually, we're very happy with it. No problems at all!

Conversation (2) *(fairly informal)*

Chris: Hi, Mark. I haven't seen you for ages. How are you?

Mark: Oh, not too good, I'm afraid.

Chris: Oh, dear! What's wrong?

Mark: Well, just a few problems at work, you know the usual.

Chris: I'm sorry to hear that.

Mark: Yes, well, I hope I can get them sorted.

Chris: Yes. Let's hope so.

Conversation (3) *(quite formal)*

Ms Trent: Good morning, Professor Trimble. It's nice to see you again.

Trimble: And you. How are things? How's Doctor Taylor doing?

Ms Trent: He's fine. He's fitted well into the team, and we're right on schedule.

Trimble: That's good.

Tips

- *How do you do?* means *Hello* or *Pleased to meet you,* whereas *How are you?* is an enquiry about how a person is feeling or the person's personal situation.
- *How are things?* is a more general enquiry, often about the job etc. in a work situation.
- When you ask about a thing like a project, you say *How's the project coming along?*
- When you ask about a person's progress, you say *How's Jim Bradshaw doing?*
- The word *Well, ...* at the beginning of a sentence is common and is used to:
  a) 'soften' a statement – *Well, jazz is quite nice, but I really prefer classical music.*
  b) give the speaker time to think – *Well, let me see, I think we can finish by Friday.*
  c) introduce something negative – *Well, I'm afraid I don't agree.*

3. Introductory Remarks: Welcoming a Visitor and Saying Goodbye

A. Welcoming a Visitor – Useful Phrases

It is important to be able to get through the first, sometimes awkward, moments of a meeting or first contact with a business partner. The following phrases should be helpful.

Good morning, Mr Goodman. Welcome **to** … (first visit)
Good morning, Bill. Nice to see you again. (subsequent visit)
How are you? (see Chapter 2)
Did you have a good journey? / How was your journey/ flight?
Did you have any problems getting here?
Is this your first visit **to** …? (if person unknown)
We're having some terrible/lovely weather at the moment.
What was the weather like in …? (where person lives)

May/Can I take your coat?
Please take a seat.
May/Can I offer you something to drink? / Would you like something to drink? / How about a coffee?

I'll just let Mr Smith know you are here. / Mr Smith will be with you in a moment.
Mr Smith will see you now.
Would you excuse me for a moment, please? / Please excuse me for a moment. (e.g. if you have to leave the office or make a phone call)
Would you come this way, please?

Asking about nationality etc.

A: Where are you from?   B: I'm from Germany.

A: Whereabouts in Germany?   B: From a small town near Stuttgart. Have you ever been to Germany?

Conversation (1)

Herr Müller:	Good morning, Mr Cox. Welcome to Hamburg. It's very nice to meet you.
Mr Cox:	Pleased to meet you.
Herr Müller:	May I take your coat?
Mr Cox:	Yes, thanks.
Herr Müller:	Please take a seat.

Herr Müller:	Is this your first visit here?
Mr Cox:	Yes, it is. I'm looking forward to it very much.
Herr Müller:	Can I offer you something to drink?
Mr Cox:	Yes, please. That would be lovely.
Herr Müller:	What would you prefer – tea, coffee or perhaps mineral water?
Mr Cox:	Coffee would be fine, thanks.

Conversation (2)

Secretary:	Good morning. Can I help you?
Ms Dubois:	Good morning. My name's Janine Dubois. I have an appointment with Mr Crane.
Secretary:	Of course, Ms Dubois. Welcome to CBI. May I take your coat? How was your flight?

Ms Dubois:	It was fine except for a bit of bad weather and turbulence.
Secretary:	Oh, dear! Well, I'm glad the weather is better here. It's lovely at the moment.
Ms Dubois:	Yes, it is, isn't it?
Secretary:	Please take a seat. I'll just let Mr Crane know you're here.
Ms Dubois:	Thank you very much.
	Secretary leaves the room.
Secretary:	Mr Crane will be with you in a moment. May I offer you something to drink?
Ms Dubois:	That would be lovely.
Secretary:	What would you prefer – tea, coffee?
Ms Dubois:	Coffee would be fine, thanks.
Secretary:	Here we are. Just help yourself to milk and sugar.
Ms Dubois:	Thanks.
Secretary:	Is this your first visit to London?
Ms Dubois:	No, I've been a few times before.
Secretary:	Well, if you have time, there are a few new sights to see.
	Phone rings.
Secretary:	Please excuse me for a moment.
	She answers the phone.
	Mr Crane will see you now, Ms Dubois. Would you come this way, please?

Conversation (3)

Steve: Hi, Ken. Nice to see you again. How are you?

Ken: Fine, thanks. And you and your family?

Steve: They're all fine, thanks. How was your flight? Everything okay?

Ken: Well, it was delayed for an hour, but other-
        wise everything was okay.

Steve: How about a coffee? Here you are. I've for-
        gotten, do you take milk and sugar?

Ken: Just milk, thanks. That's great.

Steve: Would you excuse me for a minute, Ken. I just
        have to make a quick phone call. Please help
        yourself to more coffee.

Ken: Thanks. And take your time. There's no rush.

Tips
- The word *please* is placed at the end of a polite request. *Can you help me, please?* But it is placed at
  the beginning of a polite invitation to do something. *Please take a seat. Please help yourself to coffee.*
- *May I …?* is more formal than *Can I …?* For
  example: *May I take your coat, Mr Smith? / Can I
  take your coat, Sue?*
- *May I offer you something to drink?* is more formal
  than *How about a coffee?*
- When you pass something to someone you say *Here
  you are* or *Here we are.*

B. Saying Goodbye

Preliminary remarks	**Responses**
(will depend on the situation)	
Well, I really enjoyed seeing the production plant.	That's good. / I'm glad.

I think the meeting was very useful.	Yes, me too.
Thank you for taking the time to see me.	It was a pleasure.
I've really enjoyed my visit.	That's good. / I'm glad.
Thanks for all your trouble.	My pleasure.
Thanks for coming.	I enjoyed it.

General remarks	**Responses**
Well, it's time I was leaving.	Right./Okay.
Well, it's time I was off. / I must be off now.	Right./Okay.
It was nice meeting you. (first meeting)	Likewise.
It was nice seeing you again. (later meeting)	Likewise.
Hope to see you again some-time.	Likewise.
I look forward to seeing you in July etc. (formal)	Likewise. / Me, too.
See you again/soon/next month etc. (more informal)	Yes. I'll look forward to that.
Have a good trip/flight back.	Thanks. (You, too.)
Take care. / All the best. (if you know someone well)	You, too. / Same to you.
Bye.	Bye.

Conversation (1)

John: Well, Sven, I think this meeting has been very useful.

Sven: Yes, me too.

John: Thanks for taking the time to explain everything in detail.

Sven: It was a pleasure.

John: Well, I think it's time I was off. It was nice seeing you again, Sven.

Sven: Likewise. Thanks for coming.

John: See you again next month.

Sven: Yes, see you then, John. Have a good flight back.

John: Thanks. All the best.

Sven: Same to you. Bye.

John: Bye, Sven.

Conversation (2)

Mr Black: Well, I really enjoyed looking round the factory. It was very interesting.

Herr Ott: That's good. I'm glad.

Mr Black: I think I must be off now, or I'll miss my flight.

Herr Ott: It was very nice meeting you, Mr Black.

Mr Black: Likewise. Hope to see you again some time.

Herr Ott: I'll look forward to that. Have a good trip back.

Mr Black: Thanks. And thanks for all your trouble. Bye.

Herr Ott: Bye.

4. Your Personal Profile

It is useful and gives you more confidence if you can say a few words about your background and job situation. These phrases will help.

Useful Phrases

Background

My name's …
I was born in …
I went to school in … / I went to primary/secondary/ grammar/comprehensive school in …
My parents came from …
I'm married with two children.
I'm married to Steve.

Training/Education

I did an apprenticeship / a training course in … (subject)
I trained as a … (job description e.g. electrician)
I went to university in Hamburg.
I studied / did a degree in physics at Birmingham University.
I did my PhD in …

Work experience

After that, I joined a small engineering company as a trainee manager.
My first job was with an advertising agency in Cologne.

At the moment I'm working for / I'm with Baker Ltd.

We're / I'm based in Southampton.

Our address is …

Our phone/fax number is … / My extension is … / Our email address is …

I've been with Smithsons **for** 10 years.

I've had this job **since** 1990.

My job involves designi**ng** new models / meeti**ng** a lot of people.

We deal mostly with foreign clients / questions about our products.

I'm responsible for sales / supply**ing** our main customers.

I report directly to Mr Ferguson. / Jim Burton's my boss. / Sue's our team leader.

Jim's a colleague of mine.

Tips

- You say *I was born in China.* (Not **I am born …*)
- *I'm married with two children* means *I'm married and I have two children.*
- *PhD* means *Doctor of Philosophy* and is equivalent to the German title Dr.
- When you talk about an activity which started in the past and is continuing into the present you say *I **have** worked here **for** 3 years* (you indicate the length of time) or *I **have** worked here **since** 2000* (you name the starting point of the activity).
- Note that if a second verb follows the verb *involve*, the second verb is in the *-ing* form, e.g. *That would involve spend**ing** a lot of money.*
- *Ltd* means *Limited Liability Company* (a company in which shareholders cannot be asked to pay debts beyond the face value of their shares). Compare *plc*

(*public limited company*, UK) and *Corp.* (*Corporation*, US) (a limited liability company whose shares can be bought by the public).

- The words *boss, chief* and *chef* are often confused. Your superior at work is your *boss*. The word *chief* is used in a business context to describe people at the highest level in a company, *chief executive*, the *chief of a company*. A *chef* is the head cook in a restaurant.

Hobbies/Leisure

I do a bit of garden**ing**/sport.
We go sail**ing**/walk**ing**/ski**ing**.
I play a bit of golf/tennis/squash.
I try to get to the gym as often as I can.
I like to spend a bit of time with my family if possible.
We go to the theatre/cinema quite a lot.
We do quite a lot of entertaining, so we're usually busy at weekends.
I'm so busy that I don't really have time to relax much.

Tips
- Activities are often described using the verb *do* + *-ing*. *I do some gardening. We do a lot of entertaining* (= invite guests to your home to eat).
- Types of sport are described using the verb *go* + *-ing* for the activity, and *play* if you mention the game. *I go swimming. He goes cycling. She plays tennis/golf/football.*
- *gym* (*gymnasium*) is normally a place where you do *gymnastics*, but it can also mean a fitness centre.

Conversation

Steve: Hi, I don't think we've met. I'm Steve Bradley.

Max: Hello, nice to meet you. I'm Max Turner.

Steve: Well, what do you think of the presentation up to now?

Max: Very interesting. Do you work for DLY Systems?

Steve: No, I'm actually with ICL. I'm in marketing.

Max: I hear they're doing very well. You must be pretty busy at the moment.

Steve: You can say that again. Still, I shouldn't complain about that! How about you?

Max: Oh, I'm with Simcom. We're not doing too badly either. To be honest, I'm looking forward to the bank holiday. It'll give me a chance to get out in the garden.

Steve: Yeah. I'm not such a keen gardener, I'm afraid. I'll probably be out on the golf course doing something for my handicap. That is if my family will let me!

Tips
- *You can say that again* is a phrase used to emphasize what someone has just said. A: *It's really hot today.* B: *You can say that again.*
- In the UK a bank holiday is a public holiday.

5. Talking about Company Profile and the Economy

You will also feel more confident if you can say a few words about your company, its products and the economy in general. The following phrases give you some of the necessary words and expressions to do this.

Useful Phrases

Organisations

My company is a subsidiary of a holding company in the telecommunications industry.

We're part of a group in the engineering business.

I work in the electronics division of a large multinational.

SMEs (small and medium-sized enterprises) are having problems at the moment.

Most utilities have been privatized.

The company was founded in …

The firm employs 50 people. / There are 50 employees. / They have a workforce of 50.

Of the 50, 15 are white-collar workers and the rest are blue-collar workers.

This firm has a good reputation as an employer.

There are four divisions in the group: cosmetics, pharmaceuticals, foodstuffs and publishing.

The group is divided into four main business areas.

We are based in … / We have several branches in … / We have subsidiaries in …

The main plant/factory is in … / Our head office is in … / Our headquarters are in …

Our main products/services are … / We have a wide range of products.

We make/produce/manufacture machine tools. / We provide financial services.

Our main/most important customers are …

We have mostly domestic but also a few foreign suppliers.

Our major competitors are …

There is a lot of foreign competition, but fortunately our product is very competitive.

We have a large share of the market. / We are market leaders in the production of …

Last year our turnover was … / We made a profit/loss of € 300 million.

We have a very forward-looking managing director / CEO.

The board will discuss the matter at Friday's board meeting if all the members are there.

Susan is head of the sales department. Before that, she was a self-employed businesswoman.

Senior executives/management need to talk more to middle management and line managers.

Tips
- *company/firm/business* all have the same meaning.
- A *subsidiary* is also known as a *daughter company*. The *holding company* can then be called a *parent company*.
- A *group* includes the *holding company* + *subsidiaries*.
- *Managing director / MD* (UK); *Chief Executive Officer / CEO* (US, also often UK); *President* (US) – these are names for the chief executive who runs a company on a daily basis.
- A typical organigram of a company can be found in the appendix.

The economy

The economy is doing well at the moment.

The economy is having problems at the moment.

We have a high rate of unemployment, which we need to reduce.

Unfortunately, unemployment is rising rather than falling.

The social systems – health, pensions and unemployment – need reforming.

The state, the employers and the unions will have to cooperate to achieve this.

The questions to consider are the reduction of taxes and also contributions for health, pensions, and social benefits such as the job seeker's allowance.

The government wants to privatize parts of the public sector.

Shares in these companies are usually popular.

Company executives have to satisfy their shareholders.

Companies who need money for investment can raise capital on the stock market/exchange.

Salaries are usually higher in the private sector than in the public sector.

The trade unions are campaigning for wage increases.

But they haven't yet reached a wage agreement.

They could go on strike if wage negotiations fail.

There are many more mergers and takeovers these days.

Unfortunately, there are also more bankruptcies. / XYZ Technologies has filed for bankruptcy.

A lot of their branches will have to close, and they will take on more part-time staff.

A large number of workers will be made redundant. /
   There will be a lot of redundancies.
The question is whether the state should subsidize / give
   subsidies to companies in trouble.

Tips

Here are several hints to help you learn new words.
When you are confronted with a lot of new words, it
makes sense to 'organize' them into meaningful
groups. You can do this in various ways:

a) Group words according to similarity, e.g. *employ,
   employer, employee, employment, unemployment* all
   have the same root and belong to the same concept.

b) Words like *stock exchange/market, share, shareholder, raise capital* are different but belong to the
   same topic.

c) Forming sentences helps you to learn words e.g. *To
   raise capital on the stock market, a company has to
   sell shares to shareholders.*

d) Write an explanation in English e.g. *subsidize –
   when the government gives money to a company, it
   subsidizes it.*

e) Translate a word e.g. *make someone redundant –*
   jmd. betriebsbedingt kündigen.

f) Write groups of opposites e.g. *employment/unem-
   ployment; rise/fall; increase/decrease.*

g) Always learn words that go together e.g. *raise capital; wage negotiations; cut costs.*

h) Start with a topic, e.g. *employment* and ask yourself which words you need to talk about this topic.

i) Learn words together with their grammatical structure including the preposition they take e.g. *suggest
   doing something; be responsible for doing something; be interested in; work for a company* etc.

Social Situations

6. Social Responses: Thanking, Giving and Getting Things, Apologizing

It makes a good impression if you can master simple common exchanges in a polite, friendly manner.

Saying "yes" and "no"

In English, you don't usually use the words *yes* and *no* on their own. This sounds too abrupt. Here are some short illustrations of how to say "yes" and "no".

Saying "yes"

A: Can I use your phone?	B: Yes, of course / certainly.
A: Do you work here?	B: Yes, I do.
A: Do you think he'll come?	B: Yes, I think so.
A: Shall I copy that for you?	B: Yes, please.
A: Is it okay to wait here?	B: Yes, that's fine.
A: Would you like some wine?	B: Yes, I'd love some.

Saying "no"

A: Could I speak to Mr Blair, please?	B: I'm afraid he's not in today.
A: Has he finished the report?	B: No, not yet.

A: Would you like some coffee?	B: Not at the moment, thanks.
A: Do you have the figures?	B: I'm afraid not.
A: Can we start the meeting an hour later?	B: I'd rather we didn't.
A: Can we meet on Monday?	B: I'm afraid that won't be possible.

Thanking

A: Thanks for all your help.	B: Don't mention it.
A: Thanks very much for waiting.	B: Not at all.
A: Thank you for your advice, I'm very grateful.	B: Not at all. It was a pleasure.
A: Thank you very much for the lift.	B: You're welcome.

Conversation

A: Could I borrow your mobile phone, please?	B: Certainly. Here you are.
A: Thanks very much.	B: You're welcome.

Giving and Getting Things

Some examples of what to say when passing and receiving things.

A: Have you seen my bag?	B: Yes, here it is.
A: Could you pass the bread, please?	B: Yes/Certainly, here you are.

A: Have you got the tickets?

B: Yes, here they are.

A: Thank you.

B: You're welcome.

Apologizing

Getting attention

A: Excuse me. Is there a post office near here?

B: Yes, go straight on and turn left at the traffic lights.

Apologizing before an event (e.g. in a bus)

A: Excuse me. Could I just get through? / Could you just let me through, please?

B: Sure. / Of course.

Apologizing in general

A: Sorry I'm late.

B: That's okay.

C: We couldn't contact you sooner. Sorry about that.

D: It doesn't matter.

E: I'm very/extremely sorry that Mr Brown isn't here.

F: Never mind. I'll see him later.

G: I apologize for not replying sooner.

H: Don't worry. It's not a problem.

I: I'm sorry to bother you, but I have an urgent question.

J: That's okay.

K: Please accept our apologies for the delay. (in a formal written communication)

Note

You can say *Sorry?/Pardon?* (BrE); *Excuse me?* (AmE) to indicate that you didn't understand something.

Tips

- When you answer "yes/no" questions like *Can you ski?*, it is polite and less abrupt to repeat the auxiliary verb. For example: *Can you ski? – Yes, I can. / No, I can't. Do you smoke? Yes, I do. / No, I don't.*
- In the expression *I'd rather you/he/she didn't* (in the **Saying "no"** section), the past tense is used to express politeness.
- *I'm afraid* 'softens' a negative statement. *I'm afraid Mr Brown is not available at the moment. I'm afraid we can't wait until Thursday.*
- *Excuse me* is used to attract attention in a restaurant / in a bus / in the street / in a shop etc. It is also used to interrupt politely in person or on the telephone.

7. Survival Language: Active Listening

It is important to be an 'active' listener, so that you can take steps to ensure that you understand what is said to you. If you do not understand **what is said**, you cannot participate **actively** in the conversation yourself. You should also be able to indicate that you are interested in what the other person is saying. The following phrases will help you to cope with these situations, as well as showing how to react to good and bad news, and how to check what you have heard (or think you have heard!).

Useful Phrases

Explaining language problems / Finding words

I'm afraid I can't explain this very clearly in English.
What's the English word for ...? (e.g. What's the English word for a machine that cuts grass?)
What do you say in English when ...? (e.g. What do you say in English when a company has to close because it has no money left?)
How do you say/pronounce this word?
What does ... mean? / What's the meaning of ...? (e.g. What does *supplier* mean?)
How do you spell ...? / How do you spell that? (after you hear a word).

Active listening

(1) Reactions to show interest / that you are listening

A: We are going to open   B: **Mm/Oh?** (interest)
   next week ...

A: ... and then we'll start recruiting.	B: **Right.** (acknowledging)
A: We expect a lot of applications.	B: **Do you?** (interest)
A: Yes, but we'll choose our applicants carefully.	B: **I see. / I understand.** (acknowledging)
A: We managed to save € 3 million.	B: **That's amazing!** (surprise)
A: He's got my old job.	B: **Really?** (surprise)
A: You have to make savings where you can.	B: **That's true. / Right. / Of course. / I know.** (agreeing)
A: It's quite warm today.	B: **Yes, it is. / I know.** (agreeing) **Do you think so?** (disagreeing)
A: He isn't very ambitious.	B: **No, he isn't. / True.** (agreeing) **Oh, I don't know.** (disagreeing)
A: I'll be in the office by 10.00.	B: **Right./Okay./Fine.** (acknowledging)

(2) Reactions to good news

A: I've finished that report you wanted.	B: **That's good. / Good. / Great!**
A: Sue was quite ill, but she feels better now.	B: **That's good. / Oh, I'm glad.**
A: We're getting married soon.	B: **Congratulations!**
A: My wife is out of hospital now.	B: **Oh, I'm pleased to hear that.**

(3) Reactions to bad news

A: I had a really bumpy flight.	B: **Oh dear! What a pity.**
A: Did you hear that Sue's in hospital?	B: **I'm (very) sorry to hear that.**
A: We can't finish the guidelines on time.	B: **I see. Well, …**
A: I'm afraid he isn't meeting our expectations.	B: **That's (very) unfortunate.**

Tips

- *Good* is usually an appropriate reaction to good news, although not on the occasion of a birthday, birth of a baby, marriage etc. Here you would say *Congratulations*.
- To express sympathy in a minor case (unpleasant flight, parking ticket etc.), you can say *What a pity*. In a more serious case (illness etc.), you can say *I'm (very) sorry to hear that*. *I see* is a fairly neutral reaction, whereas *That's unfortunate* is more negative.

Conversation

John: Well, the bank has finally given us the go-ahead to set up the company.

Chris: That's great!

John: So, we can start looking for premises as soon as possible.

Chris: Right.

John: They've agreed to lend us € 100,000 as start-up capital.

Chris: Have they? That's amazing!

> John: But, as you know, we'll have to put up some capital of our own.
> Chris: I know. That's the problem.
> John: Oh dear! Don't you have any cash available?
> Chris: Not right now. I will have some in a couple of months.
> John: I see. Well, we'll have to see what we can do.

Useful Phrases for Various Problems

How to check and confirm information

The following strategies may be useful in all types of communication – meetings, negotiations, telephoning, conferences etc.

a) If you did not **hear** something properly, you can say:

Sorry? (BrE)   Pardon me? (AmE)
Pardon? (BrE)   Excuse me? (AmE)

Or you can explain the problem and ask for a repetition:

(I'm) sorry, I didn't (quite) catch that/what you said.
(I'm) sorry, I missed that last part.
Could you say that again, please?
Could you go over that again, please?
Would you mind going over that again, please?

b) If you did not **understand** something, you can use the above strategy as follows:

(I'm) sorry, I don't (quite) follow you.
(I'm) sorry, I don't (quite) see what you mean.

Could you go over that again, please?
Could you put that more simply, please?

c) If you want to **interrupt** politely, you can say:

Excuse me. May I just interrupt for a second, please?
Excuse me. May I ask a question, please?
Excuse me. Would you mind if I asked a question, please?

d) If you would like **something explained in more detail**, you can say:

What exactly does … mean?
What exactly do you mean by …?
Could you explain … in a bit more detail, please?

e) If you want to **check that you understood** something correctly, you can say:

Let me just check. You said we should start the project next month. Is that right?
Did you say the end of <u>January</u>?
You <u>did</u> say January, didn't you?
Excuse me. Was that fif<u>teen</u> or fif<u>ty</u> million euros?

Note
The underlined words (or parts of a word) are stressed.

f) If you want to be **certain that you understood something**, you can summarize the contents in your own words:

Could I just go over the main points again?
Let me just check that I have understood everything correctly.
In other words, you will email the details as soon as you have them.

By that you mean that the next few weeks will be critical.

g) If you want to **correct** what someone said, you can say:

Excuse me. Not seven<u>teen</u>. <u>Seventy</u>.

Sorry, I think there's a mistake there. It should be ..., not ...

h) If you want to **make a note** of something, you can say:

Could you just repeat that (slowly), so that I can make a note, please?

Can I just make a note of that, please?

> **Tip**
> Do not hesitate to interrupt someone if you are unsure of what was said or if you did not understand what was said. You can always use the phrase *Excuse me* to interrupt politely, to ask a question or to check what someone said.

Conversation

Jack:	Hi, Michel. How are things?
Michel:	Fine, thanks. And with you?
Jack:	Okay. Michel, I'm calling about the Asian Project. How did the feasibility study go?
Michel:	It was fine. We hope to have the results by the thirteenth.
Jack:	Sorry, was that the thir<u>teenth</u> or the thir<u>tieth</u>?
Michel:	The thir<u>teenth</u>.
Jack:	Right. If all goes well, you can start building a prototype, then run some tests, and ...

Michel:	Excuse me, Jack, I didn't catch that last part.
Jack:	I said after you build the prototype, you can do some tests.
Michel:	Yes, and we do have the ML 68, you know.
Jack:	Mm. What exactly do you mean by ML 68?
Michel:	That was the prototype for the Stanford project. We can use that as a basis.
Jack:	Good. Michel, can you contact Bill Bradshaw on 01782 – that's the area code – 497563 to let him know what's happening?
Michel:	Can you just repeat that, so that I can make a note, please?

Note

You contact or reach someone **on 736542** (telephone number): *You can reach us on 233546.*

8. Starting a Conversation

You may find yourself in a situation where you have to make casual conversation which requires a bit more than the usual *How are you?* The following phrases will help you to start such a conversation. The topics are indicated in the headings.

Useful Phrases

The weather

Comment/Question	Response
What's the weather forecast like for today?	It said it was going to be warm.
Nice day, isn't it?	Yes, it's lovely.
Awful day, isn't it?	Yes, terrible.
It's very warm/hot/cold/humid/icy, isn't it?	Yes, it is.
Is it always so cold at this time of year?	Yes, as a rule. / No, this is rather exceptional.
What was the weather like in …?	Similar to here. / It was warmer/colder etc. than here.

Tips
- *It said* is a reference to something you came across in a newspaper or on the radio/TV.
- The tag *isn't it?* is an invitation to another person to continue a conversation. Other examples are: *He lives in Paris, doesn't he? He's finished work, hasn't he? You worked in Munich, didn't you? They can come, can't they?*

The occasion/event (also journey, hotel etc.)

Question	Response
Are you enjoying the con-ference / exhibition / trade fair / your visit to …?	Very much, thanks. It's very interesting / useful / informative etc.
Have you been to … be-fore?	Yes, I have. I was here about two years ago. / No, this is my first trip here.
Do you know anyone / many people here?	Yes, I've met several people before. / No, I'm meeting lots of new people.
How was your flight / trip here?	It was fine. / The flight was a bit bumpy, but otherwise it was fine.
Did you have any trouble getting here?	Well, actually, we got stuck in a traffic jam. / No, but we couldn't find a parking-space.
What's your hotel like? / Is the hotel okay?	It's fine/excellent. / Well, the service/room etc. could be better.
So, what do you think of Madrid?	It's wonderful/beautiful/ lovely / very interest-ing.
How long are you staying?	I'll be here for five days.
Are you planning to do any sightseeing?	Well, I think I might visit … / Unfortunately, I won't have time to do any sightseeing.

So, what are you doing this evening?	I think I might have a look at … / I'll probably eat in the hotel and have an early night.

> **Tips**
> - Criticism is usually expressed more indirectly in English. Thus it is better to say *The room could be better / The room isn't very good* than to say *The room's bad*.
> - The auxiliary verb *might* indicates that something is possible. It means 'will perhaps': *Perhaps it will rain = It might rain*.
> - *have an early night* means 'go to bed early'.

Casual conversation e.g. during a meeting

Comment/Question	Response
This is just what I need. (e.g. a coffee)	Yes, me too.
How's work? Are you very busy?	Yes, as usual! / Well, things are rather quiet at the moment.
How are you getting on with …? (e.g. a new process/project etc.)	It's going very well. / Actually, we did have a few teething troubles, but things are okay now.

Reference to family / other colleagues

Question	Response
How is your wife / are the children?	She's fine / They're fine, thanks.

| By the way, how is David doing? | Very well. / He's settled in now. |
| Have you seen/talked to … recently? | Yes, I saw him/her a few weeks ago. |

Reference to news / current affairs / sport etc. (e.g. in the newspaper / on TV)

Comment/Question	Response
I see that ABC Football Club is in trouble.	Really? I didn't know that. / Yes, I know.
Did you see/read that XYZ Technologies are cutting 2,000 jobs?	Are they? That's bad news. / Yes, I saw/read about that.
Did you hear about that scandal involving the ABC Bank?	No. What's it about? / Yes, isn't it awful?
It said in the paper that Mr X has been sacked.	Has he? Why? / Yes, I know.
It was on TV that the government is going to cut pensions for public employees.	Are they? That won't be very popular. / Yes, I saw that, too. Do you think they're serious?

Tips
- *have teething troubles* refers to the problems that sometimes occur **at the beginning** of a project or a production line etc. in the same way as babies *have teething troubles* when getting their first teeth.
- The concept *dismiss workers* can be expressed in other ways depending on the context: *sack/fire a worker* (informal) often indicates that the employer is dissatisfied with the worker in some way.

- *make workers redundant* indicates that the employer no longer needs the workers or is no longer able to pay them.
- *cut,* in a business context, often means 'reduce', e.g. *cut jobs/costs/pensions.*

9. Invitations and Restaurant Language

Entertaining (taking business partners to lunch/dinner) is an important aspect of business relations. The following typical restaurant language/situations will help you to feel at ease in the role of guest or host.

Useful Phrases

Invitations

Questions/Remarks	Suitable Response (yes/no)
I'd / We'd like to invite you to dinner this evening.	Thank you, I'd be delighted. / That would be lovely, but I can't make it tonight.
Would you like to join me for dinner?	I'd love to. / I'd love to, but I have to leave very early tomorrow morning.
How about lunch tomorrow?	I'd like that. / I'm sorry, but I've got another engagement.
Where/When shall we meet?	Let's meet outside the restaurant at 7.00. / I'll pick you up at your hotel at 6.30.

In the bar

What would you like to drink?	I'll have a gin and tonic, please. / I'll just have an orange juice, please.

What can I get you?	I'll have a beer, please. / I'll have a glass of red wine, please.
Let me get these.	Okay, thanks. / No, these are on me.

In the restaurant

Arriving (guest speaking to waiter)	**Waiter**
Good evening. We've ordered a table for four. The name's …	Certainly, sir/madam. Would you come this way, please?
Could we have another table, please?	Of course. / I'm afraid we're booked up.

Making clear who is paying	**Guest**
You're my/our guest this evening.	Thank you very much.
We'd like to invite you this evening.	

Ordering	**Waiter**
Excuse me. (when attracting the waiter's attention)	
Could we have the menu / wine list, please?	Certainly. / Of course.
Could we order, please?	
We'd like to order now, please.	

I'll have soup as a starter.

So, that's soup to start with. And your main course, madam?

We'd like some dessert, please.

Certainly.

Recommending

Reply

What would you recommend?

Well, the fish is usually very good here.

What can you recommend?

Well, I'd recommend the venison.

Offering

Guest (accepting and declining)

Would you like the steak?

That sounds good. / Yes, I'd like that.

How about some red wine?

Yes, that would be very nice.

Would you like some more meat?

Yes, please. / No, thank you, I'm fine.

Can I give you some more wine?

Yes, that would be very nice. / I'm fine, thanks.

Can I give you some more dessert?

It's delicious, but I don't think I could eat/manage any more.

During the meal

Reply

Could you pass the salt, please?

Of course. / Certainly.

Excuse me, is there any more water?

Yes, of course. / I'm afraid not. I'll order some more.

How's your meal?	Excellent, thanks. And yours?
How's the fish?	Fine thanks. / It's very good.
Is everything okay?	Yes, fine.

Paying	**Reply**
Could we have the bill, please?	Yes, of course.
Do you accept Visa?	Certainly.
I think there's a mistake here.	I'm sorry.

Thanking and leaving	**Reply**
Thank you for a really lovely meal.	I'm glad you enjoyed it.
Thank you for a lovely evening.	I enjoyed it very much, too.
Well, are we ready to go?	Yes, I think so.
Thanks once again.	It was a pleasure. See you again soon. Bye.

> **Tips**
> - The response *I'd love to* in answer to the question *Would you like to join me for dinner?* really means *I'd love to join you,* but it is not necessary to repeat *join you.* This is the usual response to such an invitation. *Would you like to come to the cinema? I'd love to.*
> - You normally refuse an invitation politely by saying *I'd love to, but …* or *I'm sorry, but …*
>   *Would you like to go to the theatre? I'd love to, but I have another engagement.*

- In the expressions *Let me get these* and *These are on me*, the word *these* refers to the drinks, and the speaker is indicating that he/she wishes to pay for the drinks.
- *Dessert* refers to the final sweet course at the end of a meal. It should not be confused with *desert* /ˈdezət/ (a large very dry sandy area e.g. Gobi Desert). *Dessert* /dɪˈzɜːt/ is stressed on the second syllable.
- A meal usually consists of three courses: *a starter, a main course* and a *dessert*.
- When declining an offer of more food, the expression *I'm fine* means *I've had enough. I don't want any more to eat.*
- If you discover a mistake in a bill (in a restaurant or elsewhere), it's usual to point this out indirectly by using an expression like *I think there's a mistake here* even if you are certain that something is wrong.

Conversation

Mr Taylor: Well, I'm glad we sorted everything out. Now, I'd like to invite you to dinner this evening.

Mr Davis: Oh, I'd be delighted. Thank you.

Mr Taylor: Do you like Italian food? There's a very good Italian restaurant near the river.

Mr Davis: That sounds good.

Mr Taylor: Right. When shall we eat? Is 7.30 okay for you?

Mr Davis: That's fine.

Mr Taylor: Okay, I'll pick you up at your hotel at 7.00.

Mr Davis: That's very kind of you. See you then.

In the bar

Mr Davis: Now, what can I get you to drink?

Mr Taylor: No, these are on me. I insist. What would you like?

Mr Davis: Well, I'll have a beer, please.

In the restaurant

Mr Taylor: Would you like to sit here?

Mr Davis: Thanks.

Mr Taylor: (*To waiter*) Excuse me. Could we have the menu, please?

Mr Davis: Everything looks very good. What can you recommend?

Mr Taylor: Well, the sole is very good, or the steak. And all the pasta dishes are good. And you must try the mixed salad. It's particularly good here. I always have carpaccio as a starter.

Mr Taylor: Are we ready to order now?

Mr Davis: Yes, I think so. I'll have asparagus to start with, and pork to follow.

Mr Taylor: Right, a good choice. What would you like to drink?

Mr Davis: Can I leave that to you?

Mr Taylor: Okay. How about a dry white wine?

Mr Davis: That would be very nice.

During the meal

Mr Taylor: How's the pork?

Mr Davis: It's excellent, thanks. And your fish?

Mr Taylor: Fine, thanks. Can I give you some more wine?

Mr Davis:	No, thanks, I'm fine. I have an early start in the morning, so I'd better not drink too much. But it's very good.
Mr Taylor:	How about a dessert? The ice cream is very good.
Mr Davis:	That would be nice, but I don't think I can manage any more.
Mr Taylor:	A coffee, then?
Mr Davis:	Yes, I'd like that.

Thanking and leaving

Mr Davis:	Well, thank you for a really lovely meal. I've enjoyed this evening.
Mr Taylor:	I enjoyed it very much, too. Are we ready to leave, then?
Mr Davis:	Yes, I think so. Thanks once again.
Mr Taylor:	It was a pleasure. Let me give you a lift back to your hotel.
Mr Davis:	That's very kind of you, thanks.

Specialist Vocabulary

menu: Speisekarte; *starter:* Vorspeise; *main course:* Hauptgericht, -gang; *venison:* Wild(bret); *to pass:* (herüber)reichen; *sole:* Seezunge; *dishes:* Speisen, Gerichte; *asparagus:* Spargel; *pork:* Schweinefleisch.

10. Getting and Giving Information and Permission

You will frequently be faced with a situation where you need to ask someone to do something for you or you want to know if you can do something. You may, on occasion, also need information or advice. You may also want to offer help, information or advice, or make a suggestion. The following phrases will help in these situations.

Useful Phrases

Asking someone to do something

Request	Response
Can you email this to my office, please?	Yes, of course. / Certainly. / I'm sorry, but …
Could you pass the coffee, please?	Of course. Here you are.
Would you mind sending this fax for me, please?	Not at all.
Would you pop into my office before you leave?	Yes, okay.
Do you think you could pick Mr Brent up from the airport?	Yes, of course. / Actually, I have a meeting then. / Sorry / I'm afraid I can't because …
You won't forget to phone John, will you?	No, I won't.

Some telephoning requests

Could I speak to ..., please?

Can I leave a message, please?

Could you ask Sue to call me back?

Could you speak more slowly, please?

Some written requests

Could you please send us your price list?

We would be very grateful if you could send us details of your new product range.

Asking for information

You say	You think
Do you know when the meeting starts?	When does the meeting start?
Could you let me know which documents you need?	Tell me which documents you need.
Do you know if he's coming to Germany?	Is he coming to Germany?
Can you tell me if we have this programme?	Do we have this programme?

Offering something / to help

Offer	Response
Would you like a coffee?	Yes, please. I'd love one. / Not at the moment, thanks.
Would you like to phone your office?	Yes, please. / No, it's okay, thanks.

Would you like **me** to phone your office?	Please, if it's no trouble. / No, it's all right, thanks.
Shall I make a copy for you?	If you don't mind. / I don't think you need to, thanks.
Can I help in any way?	That's very kind of you. /
Can I be of any help?	No, it's okay, thanks.

On the telephone / In writing

Please do not hesitate to get in touch if we can be of any help.

Asking for permission to do something

Request	**Response**
Can I use your computer?	Of course, go ahead. / I'm afraid not, because …
Could I interrupt for a moment, please?	Certainly, go ahead. / If I could just finish.
Do you mind if I wait here?	Not at all.
Is it all right if I phone later?	Of course. No problem.

Giving advice

Advice	**Response**
I think you should call a meeting.	Okay, I'll think about it. / I'm not sure.
If I were you, I'd speak to him.	You could be right. / Maybe.

It might be a good idea to cancel the order.	Perhaps we should. / Do you think so?
Make sure you read the small print.	Yes, of course.

Making suggestions

Suggestion	Response
I suggest that we postpone the meeting.	I completely agree. / I'm afraid I don't agree at all.
I would suggest postponing a decision.	I agree. / I don't think I can go along with that.
Why don't we raise our prices?	That might be a good idea. / I don't think that's such a good idea.
How about starting a new advertising campaign?	That's a possibility. / We could do that, but …
We could cut our costs.	I agree up to a point, but … / That might be difficult.
What if we cut the number of jobs?	Perhaps. / Well, we can think about it.

Tips
- The expression *Would you mind …* is followed by a verb in the *-ing* form. *Would you mind sending this fax?*
- The **positive** answer to questions with the verb *mind* (*Would you mind waiting? / Do you mind if I use your phone?*) is *Not at all*.
- The verb *pop in/into* means to go somewhere very

briefly. *Would you pop into the kitchen and turn the cooker off, please?*

- In the **Asking for information** section, the left-hand column shows the indirect and polite way of asking the direct question in the right-hand column.
- Compare the two sentences: *Would you like to phone your office? / Would you like* **me** *to phone your office?* The first sentence is an offer to allow someone to phone his/her office. In the second sentence, **you** offer to make the call **yourself**.
- The expression *if it's no trouble* means 'if this is not difficult for you'.
- The verb *suggest* can be followed by *that* or a verb in the *-ing* form. *I suggest that we call a meeting. / I suggest calling a meeting.*
- The expression *I can go along with that* means 'I can accept that'.

Conversation

Dave:	Sue, can you email all the invitations to our annual conference?	**Request**
Sue:	Of course. Shall I let you know when everyone has answered?	**Response + Offer to help**
Dave:	No, it's all right. Do you know if Steve has arranged a venue?	**Response + Asking for information**
Sue:	I'm not sure. Here he is now.	
Dave:	Ah, Steve. How are things going? Can you tell me if the venue for the conference is sorted out?	**Asking for information**

Steve:	Well, almost. I would suggest using the new conference centre.	**Suggestion**
Dave:	We could do that, but wouldn't it be rather expensive?	**Response**
Sue:	If I were you, I'd take our usual hotel again.	**Advice**
Steve:	Okay, I'll think about it. Would you like me to arrange accommodation for the delegates, too?	**Response + Offer to help**
Sue:	No, it's okay, thanks. They're arranging their own accommodation.	**Response**
Dave:	Well, I think that's all for the moment. Make sure you keep an eye on the schedule so that we don't forget anything.	**Advice**

Business Communication

11. Meetings

It is essential to be able to cope with meetings held in English. You may have to chair the meeting yourself, or you may want to play a more active role. Knowing the fixed expressions common to such meetings is a great help (see below). You should also remember that if you are not following the discussion, you cannot make any useful contributions, so no-one will mind if you interrupt to ask for something to be repeated or explained.

Useful phrases	**Useful sentences**
You **arrange/fix** a meeting.	We've fixed the meeting for Friday.
You **have/are at** a meeting.	I had three meetings yesterday. / I was at three …
You **are in** a meeting now.	I'm afraid Mr Trent isn't available. He's in a meeting.
You can **postpone** a meeting.	I'm afraid we will have to postpone Tuesday's meeting.
You can **reschedule** a meeting.	They've rescheduled the meeting for next week.
You can **cancel** a meeting.	They've cancelled the meeting altogether.
You can **adjourn** a meeting.	We decided to adjourn the meeting till tomorrow.
You **draw up an agenda** which lists the **items** for discussion.	My boss has drawn up the agenda, but I think there are too many items.

The first item is often **'matters arising'** (from the last meeting).	So, let's deal with matters arising first.
The last item is often **'any other business'** (items not on the agenda).	Well, if we all agree on that, is there any other business?
You may **circulate** the agenda to the **participants**.	Have you circulated the agenda to all the participants?
Someone will **chair** the meeting. This is the **chairman/chairwoman/chairperson**.	Who's chairing the meeting?
Someone will **take the minutes**.	Have you read the minutes of our last meeting?

Getting through a Meeting

Starting the meeting

Right./Okay. May I have your attention, please? (If everyone is still talking and you want to start.)
Good morning, ladies and gentlemen / everyone.
Thank you / Thanks for coming.
So, shall we make a start?
First of all, I'd like to introduce our colleagues from Milan. (If unknown colleagues are present.)

Opening remarks

Have you all got a copy of the agenda?
The meeting is scheduled to finish at …
John will take the minutes.

I'd like to go through the items as they are listed on the
    agenda.
Is that okay with everyone?
Right. Now, the purpose of this meeting is to …
Okay. As you know, we're here today to …

Reporting

I'd just like to fill you in on the current situation.
Can I just say a word or two about the current situation?

Moving to the first point

Let's start with item one. / Let's start by discussing the
    new schedule.
Now, we need to discuss …

Moving to the next point

Right. Let's move on to the next point.
Could we move on to item three?

Handing over to another person

I'd like to hand over to Michael. He'll tell us about … /
    He'll brief us on …
I'd like to bring John in at this point / here.

Asking for opinions

How do you feel about that, Peter?
Any views on that, Mr Riley?
What do you think?
Would anyone like to comment on that? / Any com-
    ments? (A question to everyone)

Giving opinions

I think that …
I would say that …
It seems to me that …
I'd like to stress that …

Asking to make a comment

Could I just comment on that?
Excuse me. Could I just say something here, please?

Agreeing/Disagreeing (ranging from strong to weak)

Agreement	Disagreement
I completely agree.	I'm afraid I don't agree at all.
I think you're right.	I'm afraid I can't agree with you on that.
I agree up to a point, but …	I don't think we can go along with that.
You may be right, but …	That might be difficult.

Interrupting

Sorry to interrupt, but …
Before you go on, could I just ask something?

Stopping interruptions

Could I just finish this point?
If I could just finish.

Asking for repetition or clarification

(1) If you didn't **hear**:

Sorry, I didn't catch what you said.
Could you repeat that, please?
Sorry, I missed that. Could you say it again, please?

(2) If you didn't **understand**:

Sorry, I don't (quite) follow you. Could you put that
   more simply, please?
Sorry, I don't (quite) see what you mean. Could you go
   over that again, please?

(3) If you want the speaker to be **more exact**:

Excuse me. What exactly do you mean by ...?

(4) If you want to **check** you understand:

So you mean ...
So what you're saying is ...
In other words, ...

Referring back

A few moments ago you mentioned ... Could you explain that again, please?
Could I go back to what you said about ...? What's the
   current situation?

Stopping people talking at once

Okay John, thanks. Any comments to make, Kate?
One at a time, please!

Keeping to the point

Could we get back to the main point, please?
I think that's outside the scope of this meeting.

Expressing doubt/misgivings

I'm still a bit unhappy with …
I can see some difficulties with that idea/date etc.

Dealing with misunderstanding

I think there seems to be some misunderstanding.
Could I just clarify what I said?

Being non-committal

It's very difficult to answer that question at the moment.
I'll have to get back to you on that.

Watching the time

There's not much time left. Could you be brief, please?
We're running out of time. Perhaps we can talk about
this later.

Dealing with outstanding issues

Now, we still need to look at … / think about …
We haven't decided yet what to do about … / how to
plan … / whether to …

Making suggestions

I'd like to suggest that we …
I'd like to make an alternative suggestion.
Why don't we …?
Can we vote on that proposal?
Who's in favour? / Who's against?

More useful phrases

It depends. / It depends on whether …
The reason for that is/was … / That's the reason why our profits fell.
This is/was due to …
That meant that …
So, as a result of that, we have to …

Summarizing

Are we all agreed on that?
Does anyone have anything to add?
Are there any more questions?
Right, to sum up then, we'll …
Okay, so we've decided to …

Delegating tasks

Steve, do you think you could …?
We need some figures on that. Can I leave that with you, Barbara?

Closing the meeting

Well, that seems to cover/be everything.
If no-one has anything else to add, we'll finish for today.

I'd like to thank Jean for being here today. (If a visitor was present.)
Thank you all for coming.
See you again at our next meeting.

Tips

- The word *schedule* ('time plan') is also a verb (*schedule, scheduled, scheduled*) and means 'plan'. *We have scheduled ten weeks for this project.* You can also *reschedule* something.
- *Agenda* is pronounced /əˈdʒendə/.
- *Matters arising* means any questions remaining/resulting from the last meeting.
- *Take the minutes* means to write down what is said at a meeting. *The minutes* are the written record.
- Many English verbs are so-called *phrasal verbs*. They consist of a verb + preposition/adverb (see above *fill someone in* and *move on*). Such a verbal expression is sometimes used with another preposition, so that one preposition may follow another. We then have sentences like *John will fill us **in on** the current situation. Could we move **on to** item two? I'd like to bring John **in at** this point.* Such a combination may sound strange, but is absolutely correct and commonly used.
- *I'll have to get back to you on that* means *I'll think about it / I'll find out about it and contact you again.* This is a commonly-used phrase in a business context.

Conversation

Steve: Good morning everyone. Thanks for coming. So, shall we make a start? (**starting**)

We're scheduled to finish at 3.00 and John's taking the minutes. Now, as you know, this meeting is about cutting costs. (**opening**)

I'd like to hand over to Mike, who's going to fill us in on the current situation. (**handing over**, **reporting**)

Mike: Right, let's start by looking at the ways we have of cutting costs. (**first point**)

I would say that cutting the research and development budget is one possibility. (**giving opinion**)

Any views on that, Joe? (**asking for opinions**)

Joe: I completely agree with you. (**strong agreement**)

Sue: You may be right, but (**weak agreement/disagreement**) it seems to me that we have a lot of other options. (**giving opinion**)

Mark: I'd like to make an alternative suggestion. Why don't we concentrate on outsourcing more functions? (**making suggestions**) For instance ...

Sue: Before you go on, could I just ask how many jobs would be lost if we did that? (**interrupting**)

Mark: Well, if I could just finish first. (**stopping interruptions**) We can outsource various functions without causing redundancies. We would only have natural wastage.

Sue: What exactly do you mean by 'natural wastage'? (**asking for clarification**)

Mark: People resigning, taking early retirement and so on.

Mike: I can see some difficulties with that. (**express-

ing doubt) Just how much would we actually save?

Mark: It's very difficult to be exact at the moment. **(being non-committal)**

Steve: We're running out of time **(watching the time)**, so I would suggest that we all go away and think about this and meet again in a week's time. **(making a suggestion)**

Are we all agreed on that? **(summarizing)**

Mark, we need some concrete figures on your suggestion. Can I leave that with you? **(delegating tasks)**

If no-one has anything to add, we'll finish for today. Thank you all for coming. **(closing)**

12. Presentations

Many things contribute to making a presentation successful – among others, interesting content, a clear structure,
good use of visuals and an enthusiastic presentation. But
all of these depend to some extent on the language you
use to guide your audience through the presentation.
This chapter will help you with the key words and
phrases you are likely to need.

Useful Phrases

Welcoming an audience / Introducing a panel or col-leagues

Good morning, ladies and gentlemen. / Good morning,
    everyone.
On behalf of …, let me welcome you to … / Thank you
    for coming.
My name's … / I'm …
I'm responsible for … / I'm in charge of …

I'd like to introduce … / Let me introduce …
It gives me great pleasure to introduce Dr Dubois from
    our Paris branch.
He's going to talk to us about …

> **Tips**
> * *Good morning everyone / Thank you for coming* are
>   more informal expressions.
> * Someone is addressed as either Mr Smith, Dr Smith
>   or Professor Smith (according to his/her title).

- *Never* say *Mr Dr Smith or *Professor Dr Smith.
- You can get the audience on your side by excusing your 'not quite perfect English'. You can say *Please excuse my English which is a bit rusty.*

Welcoming people you know

Nice to see you all again.
Nice/Good to see you again, Bill. How are you? / How are things?

Making a start

Today, we want to think about / look at … (more informal)
As you know, I'm here to talk about …
Now, I've been asked to tell you something about … (more formal)

Referring to questions

Can I just say that if anyone has a question, please feel free to interrupt.
Can I just say that if you have any questions, I'll be glad to answer them at the end.
Can I just say that if you have any questions, there'll be time at the end to answer them.

Explaining the situation

The purpose of this presentation is to …
The current situation is as follows …
As you know, we need to look at …
I just want to say a few words about … (more informal)
I just want to tell you a bit about … (more informal)

Structuring talk/presentation

I'll begin by describing ... / showing you ... / explaining ... / telling you ...
Then I'll go on to ...
Finally, I'll ...

> **Tip**
> A verb following a preposition like *by* is in the *-ing* form: *You learn by doing* (see also Chapter 1).

First point

The first thing I'd like to do is explain to you why ... / talk about ...
So, I'd like to begin by explaining to you why ... / talking to you about ...
Firstly/First, ... Secondly/Second, ...
To start with, let me say that ... / I'd like to say that ... / I want to say that ...

> **Tips**
> • When introducing a list of points, you say *First/ Firstly*, not *At first*.
> • You *explain* something *to* a person.

Next point

Now, I'd like to move on to ... / Now, moving on to ...
Now, I'd like to turn to ... / Now, turning to ...
Now, we come to ...

> **Tip**
> *I'd like to turn to* indicates that you are changing direction.

Visual aids

If you look at this transparency, you can see ...
This transparency shows ...
As you can see from this overhead, ...
I have prepared an overhead to illustrate this.
This graph/diagram/figure/flow chart shows that/how/
    why ...

(Once the audience's attention has been directed to the
transparency)
We can see here that ...
Here we can see that ...
Notice here that ...

Types of diagram used in transparencies

graph (vertical axis, horizontal axis), curve, figure, bar
chart, flow chart, pie chart, table, diagram, pictogram, organigram, solid line (___), broken line (_ _), dotted line
(......)

Equipment

overhead projector, plug, socket/power point, transpar-
ency/overhead, digital projector, slide, flip chart, pointer,
marker pen, board

> **Tip**
> Notice that *an overhead* is also used for *a transpar-
> ency.*

Emphasizing a point

The main/essential/crucial point is ...

Making suggestions

I/We would suggest changing/buying/monitoring etc.
We would advise changing/buying/monitoring etc.

> **Tip**
> If a verb follows *suggest* or *advise,* it is in the *-ing*
> form: *We would advise changing the process.* (Compare *involve doing* in Chapter 4).

Referring back

As I said at the beginning, ...
As I've already said, ...
As I mentioned earlier, ...

Referring to what you will say

I'll come to that later.
I'll talk about this later.

Interrupting

May I just interrupt here for a second?
Could I just ask a question?

> **Tip**
> Dealing with interruptions has been included here, because when giving a more informal presentation, you may be faced with interruptions.

Stopping interruptions

If I could just finish this point.

Summarizing

So, to sum up, …
So now I just want to summarize the main points again.
We've looked at …

Finishing

My final point is …
In conclusion, let me say that … / could I just say that …
So, I think that covers most of the points / everything.
  (more informal)

Thank you all for coming.
Thank you for your attention.

Dealing with questions

Understanding the question
(Rephrasing the question)
If I understand the question correctly, you would like to
  know …

(Clarifying the question)
When you say … do you mean …?

(Asking for repetition)
Sorry, could you repeat the question, please?

Giving an opinion
I/We think that …
I would say that …
Well, as I see it, …

Agreeing with the questioner

Yes, I agree.
That's a good point.
That fits in with what I said about …

Disagreeing with the questioner

Yes, I see your point, but … / Yes, but … / Perhaps, but …
Still / All the same, …
On the other hand, …
I don't think that would work.
I don't think so.

Replying if you don't know the answer

I'm afraid I don't have the answer to that at the moment.
It's difficult to say.
I'd have to check on that.

Asking a question (pinpointing the reference)

You mentioned …
Could I go back to the point you made about …?
Could I go back to what you said about …?
What's your view of that?
What's the current situation?
Could you explain that in more detail?
Could you give us some more information on that?

A short presentation of Zillkon GmbH

Good morning everyone. On behalf of Zillkon Ltd, let me welcome you to this presentation. My name's Wolfgang Zillgitt and I'm the managing director.

I just want to say a few words about our relatively new and innovative company. I'll begin by describing the sort of products manufactured by Zillkon, and their purpose. Then I'll give you some information about the company's background and its customers, and finally, we'll see how the company sees its future. Can I just add that if you have any questions, I'll be glad to answer them at the end.

So, to start with, let's look at Zillkon's main products. Zillkon manufactures devices to reduce radiated electromagnetic interference. This might be better known to you as electro-smog.

Devices which reduce this are known as shielding devices. As you can see from this overhead, such devices are in the form of gaskets. Electromagnetic interference, or EMI, is electro-magnetic radiation which can adversely affect the performance of electrical circuits in any form of electrical equipment from small domestic appliances like toasters to electronic equipment in planes. This EMI may be external interference from other electrical devices, or emissions from sources inside equipment which can affect other circuits within the same equipment. This overhead illustrates the phenomenon. Notice here (*pointing to overhead*) that EMI shielding is installed at gaps in the housings of electronic equipment where EMI can both escape and enter. As I mentioned above, the shielding is used to seal these gaps and is usually in the form of gaskets.

Now, I'd like to turn to the history of the company. We founded Zillkon in March, 1995 and we are based just outside Berlin. The company has 22 employees and, within a very short time, has developed into the largest producer of copper-beryllium gaskets in Germany.

We deliver to customers in the German market and in the European market, for example, the UK, Switzerland, Denmark and others, as well as to Japanese customers. Some of our most important customers are IBM, Siemens and Philips.

Zillkon's products are used widely in the fields of high-frequency technologies, measuring and controlling technologies, nuclear physics, air and space travel and electronic data-processing. I would like to stress that one of our main strengths is our ability to work to the specifications of individual customers.

Now we come to strategies for the future. Zillkon is currently co-operating with various scientific and technological institutions, as well as with suppliers, to develop innovative and improved products using new materials with the aim of extending their existing product range.

In conclusion, can I just say that I hope you found this presentation useful and informative, and I'd like to thank you for coming today.

Now, does anyone have a question?

Specialist Vocabulary

device: Vorrichtung, Gerät; *radiated electromagnetic interference:* Störung(en) durch elektromagnetische Strahlung (*to radiate:* strahlen); *shielding:* Abschirmung, Schutz; *gasket:* Dichtung; *adversely:* nachteilig; *to affect:* beeinflussen, beeinträchtigen; *circuits:* Schaltkreise, Stromkreise; *domestic appliances:* elektrische (Haushalts-)Geräte; *housing:* Gehäuse; *to seal the gap:* den Spalt, die Lücke schließen, abdichten; *copper-beryllium:* Kupfer mit Berylliumlegierung; *to measure:* messen.

13. Negotiations

A negotiation is a discussion – something like a meeting – but between people with different interests. Some of the language you need is like the language for meetings. So general activities which occur in any discussion – like *Asking for opinions, Giving opinions, Agreeing/Disagreeing, Interrupting, Stopping interruptions, Making suggestions* – can be found in Chapter 11, **Meetings**. Other activities from the chapter on **Meetings** which are particularly relevant to negotiations will be touched on here. You also need language for problem-solving and reaching a compromise. The following phrases should help to guide you through negotiations.

Useful Phrases	**Useful Sentences**
You can **set up** negotiations.	We have set up negotiations to start next month.
You can **take part in** negotiations.	Who is taking part in the negotiations?
You can **adjourn** negotiations.	We had to adjourn because we ran out of time.
You can **break off** negotiations.	We got bogged down, so we had to break off negotiations.
You can **resume** negotiations.	We hope to resume negotiations next week.
You can **take a timeout**.	We reached a stalemate, so we took a timeout.

Tips
- *We got bogged down* means 'We were unable to continue'. One reason may be that you are paying too much attention to details.
- *We reached a stalemate* means 'We reached a situation where neither side could win or take any action'. This phrase comes from the game of chess.

Getting through Negotiations

Starting the negotiations

Right. May I have your attention, please? (If people are still talking)

Good morning, everyone. Welcome to ... I hope you all had a good journey.

Sorry about this depressing weather. / You've brought some nice weather with you.

So, shall we make a start? I'm sure we'll have very successful discussions.

Tip
The above remarks are intended to create rapport. There are of course others you can use.

Moving to the first phase

Perhaps we can begin by making our position clear.
Our aim is to ...
Our main priority is to ...

Making a concrete proposal

We suggest buying/selling/investing ...
We propose offering/delivering/paying ...
What we are proposing is to build the plant ourselves.

Seeking approval

How does that sound?
Are you happy with that?
Would that be acceptable?
Could you go along with that?

Identifying a problem

I think the main problem seems to be the delivery schedule.
The main problem seems to be that we would need more time.

Referring back

A few moments ago, you mentioned ... Could we look at that again, please?
Could I go back to what you said about an exclusivity clause?

Asking for repetition or clarification

(1) If you didn't **hear**:

Sorry, I didn't catch what you said. Could you repeat that, please?
Sorry, I missed that. Could you say it again, please?

(2) If you didn't **understand**:

Sorry, I don't (quite) follow you. Could you put that more simply, please?

Sorry, I don't (quite) see what you mean. Could you go over that again, please?

(3) If you want the speaker to be **more exact**:

Excuse me. What exactly do you mean by ...?

(4) If you want to **check** you understand:

So you mean ...

So what you're saying is ...

In other words, ...

Expressing doubt/misgivings

I'm still a bit unhappy with ...

I can see some difficulties with that idea/date etc.

I'm afraid that's not feasible.

Dealing with misunderstanding

I think there seems to be some misunderstanding.

Could I just clarify what I said?

Being non-committal

It's very difficult to answer that question at the moment.

I'll have to get back to you on that.

Referring to higher authority

I don't have the authority to agree to that. I'll have to check and get back to you.

Reacting positively to a proposal

We might be able to agree to that.
That sounds reasonable.

Making a counter-proposal

Well, what if we ...? (What if we allowed six weeks for
   delivery?)
Supposing we ...? (Supposing we allowed six weeks for
   delivery?)
We would prefer to ...

> **Tips**
> • *Supposing* (also *suppose*) means the same as *What
>   if* ...
> • The above phrases are followed by the past tense,
>   which makes the request less definite. The present
>   tense can also be used: *What if we offer more com-
>   mission?*

Bargaining

What would you do if suppliers increased their prices?
What do you normally do in a situation like this?
How do you normally test the finished product?
What if supplies run out?

> **Conversation**
> A: If you order 500 items, we'll give you a 10% dis-
>   count.
> B: How much would you give us if we ordered more?
> A: If you ordered more than 1,000, we'd give you 15%.

B: What if we paid in advance? Would you increase our discount?

A: I'm afraid that wouldn't be feasible.

Tip

Notice the use of tenses in conditional sentences (*If-*sentences). The present tense is used to talk about a real or probable situation in the future. *If you order 500 items, we'll give you a 10% discount.* The past tense is used to talk about a hypothetical situation now or in the future. *If we ordered more, would you give us a higher discount?*

Pattern: *If you **order** ..., we **will** give ...; If you **ordered** ..., we **would** give ...*

Making a concession

We would be willing to accept your terms, if you gave us an order for 1,000 items.

We could lower the price, if you increased your order.

Accepting an offer

That seems to be acceptable/satisfactory.

We can accept that.

We can go along with that.

Rejecting an offer outright (compare "expressing doubt")

I'm afraid we can't accept that.

I'm afraid that's unacceptable.

I'm sorry, but that would be out of the question.

> **Tip**
> It is more polite to be indirect when disagreeing. Disagreement can be softened by beginning with *I'm afraid* and by using *would*. For example: *I'm afraid that would be rather difficult.*

Summing up

Shall we just go over what we have agreed on so far?
So, let's just summarize what we have agreed on.

Reaching an agreement

Well, we seem to agree on everything.
Is everyone happy with this agreement?

Closing

Well, I'd like to thank everyone for making these negotiations so successful.
Well everyone, thank you for all your efforts. I think we've achieved a lot today.
Well, that seems to cover everything. Thank you for coming today. (less formal)

Adjourning negotiations

It might be a good idea to adjourn to a later date.
What about meeting again at a later date?

Breaking off negotiations

I don't think we can achieve anything by continuing at the moment.
Perhaps we can continue at a later date.

Interrupting negotiations

This might be a suitable point to take a timeout. Is that okay with everyone?

Perhaps we should take a break at this point.

Successful negotiations – Selling a house

Estate agent:	Good morning, Mr and Mrs Felton. Lovely morning, isn't it?
Prospective buyers:	Yes, it is. About time the weather improved a bit.
Estate agent:	Now, you've had a look round the property. How do you feel about it?
Buyers:	Well, we like it and we're interested. But we think the price is a bit too high.
Estate agent:	Of course, the sellers would be prepared to discuss that. But, I'll have to check with them and get back to you.
	Several days later
Estate agent:	Nice to see you both again. So, I've had a word with Mr and Mrs Curry and they are prepared to drop the price by £1,000 if you agree to close the sale within the next week. Would that be acceptable?
Buyers:	I'm afraid that's just not feasible. We can't sell our present house for another few months. In any case, we would prefer to wait

	and see how the surveyor values the house.
Estate agent:	Okay. Let's wait for the survey and take it from there.
	Several days later
Estate agent:	Well, as you can see from the survey, there are a few minor repairs to be done. If Mr and Mrs Curry reduced the asking price by £2,000, which would include the cost of repairs, would you be prepared to agree to a quick sale? You could move into the house at any time. How does that sound?
Buyers:	That doesn't sound too bad, but we're still a bit unhappy with the price.
Estate agent:	What if the carpets were included in the offer? Could you go along with that?
Buyers:	That sounds reasonable. We can accept that.
Estate agent:	Great! I'll put all the details in writing and wait for your confirmation, and then we can close the sale.

14. Showing Visitors around your Company

You may occasionally be required to show a visitor around your company. This can vary from a brief tour for visitors who are familiar with your business to a more detailed tour for visitors who are new to the company, or even tours for members of the public. You may have to give details of the company background, product range, competitors, current projects and so on, as well as show the visitor(s) the actual production plant. The following phrases should be helpful.

Useful Phrases

Welcoming visitors

Good morning, ladies and gentlemen. / Good morning, everyone.

On behalf of ..., I'd like to welcome you to this tour of our factory/plant.

My name's ..., and I'll be showing you round this morning.

My name's ..., and I'm in charge of / responsible for ...

> **Tip**
> If you only have one visitor, you can use some of the phrases from Chapter 3.

Outlining stages of the tour

Let me tell you what we have arranged for today ... How does that sound?

I'd like to start by telling you a little about ...

Then we'll move on to …
And finally, we'll have a look at …
Can I start by filling you in on the background of our
   company?

Questions

Please don't hesitate to ask any questions as we go along.
Does anyone have a question?
Would anyone like to ask a question?

Background (see also Chapter 5)

The company was founded in 1980 and has since grown
   to become one of the main producers of … in this
   country.
This company is part of a group in the pharmaceuticals
   business.
We are a subsidiary of …

We are based in Milan, but have 50 branches worldwide.
This factory/plant employs 2,000 people. / We have a
   workforce of 2,000.
Our turnover last year was …

Products/Markets (see also Chapter 5)

Our main products/services are …
We manufacture and sell information processing prod-
   ucts.
We are the market leader in data storage products.
Our main export markets are in Asia.
Most of our customers are in the domestic market.
We have a market share of 30%.

Current projects

We are currently co-operating with partners in America
   on several joint ventures.

We are currently restructuring the business to enable us
   to develop new products.

We are expanding our activities in the field of entertain-
   ment.

We are currently developing a new drug for the treatment of heart disease.

> **Tip**
> Notice the use of tenses. The simple present (*This
> plant employs … / We sell …*) is used for permanent
> situations / routine activities which may apply to the
> past, present or future. The simple continuous (*We
> are co-operating … We are expanding …*) is used to
> describe activities happening at the moment (*cur-
> rently*).

Stages of the tour

Starting

Let's start by looking at …
First, we'll have a look at …

Describing places

Now, here you can see …	in front of
Here we are in …	behind
We are now in …	on the right/left
This is where we …	next to / opposite
That building over there is where …	

Moving on

If you would follow me, please.
Would you come this way, please?
Let's move on to …
Perhaps we can go on to …
Now I'd like to show you …

Regulations

I'm afraid mobile phones / mobiles are not allowed in here.
I'm afraid this is a no-smoking area.
We have to wear helmets / protective clothing here.

Last stage

Finally, let's take a look at …
So, the last thing/place I'd like to show you is …

Concluding the tour

Well, I think that's about it. (more informal)
Well, that concludes our tour.
Well, I think you have seen everything of interest.
I hope you found it interesting.
I hope you enjoyed it.

Pointing out things of interest

As you can see, …
An interesting fact is that …
This is of special interest, because …
This is especially effective/difficult/costly/time-consuming/complicated etc.
Notice in particular that …
Notice here that …

Describing a process

First, we...
To start with, ...
Then, ...
Next, ...
After that, ...
The next step is to ...
Finally, ...

Specialist vocabulary

drug: Medikament; *treatment:* Behandlung; *helmet:* Helm; *protective clothing:* Schutzkleidung; *to screw:* (ver)schrauben; *to polish:* polieren, schleifen.

A tour of the Spode pottery factory

Good morning, ladies and gentlemen. On behalf of Spode, I'd like to welcome you to our factory. My name's Jill Smith, and I'll be showing you round today.

I'd like to start by telling you a little about the history of our company. Then we'll move on to the production area, where we will look at the production of certain pieces of pottery and how they are decorated, fired and glazed.

This company was founded by Josiah Spode in 1776 and is the oldest English pottery company still operating on its original 9-acre site, with some of the original buildings still standing. It has, of course, since become famous throughout the world and has customers world-wide. You can see the development of ceramics at Spode in our museum. There are items from the early years of Spode as well as designs for the royal family and Spode designs for the 21st century on display there. Two of the most important developments in the ceramics industry occurred at Spode. These were the perfection of underglaze blue printing and the invention of bone china.

So, if you would like to come this way, we'll start with the first stage in the production of pottery. Please don't hesitate to ask any questions you may have as we go along.

As you probably know, the main raw material used in pottery production is clay. Spode's famous bone china is made by adding up to 50% animal bone to the clay mix. We are now in the workshop where the clay is prepared. Over there you can see the sieves which remove solid particles from the clay. After drying, we are left with large slabs of semi-dry clay, which are then further dried in this machine called a pug-mill to produce uniformly-shaped rolls.

Now I'd like to show you two of the main processes used in producing different types of ceramics. First we'll look at casting – a process used to produce holloware, such as vases, cups and coffee pots. Here you can see clay slip – that's a thin mixture of clay and water – being poured into a mould for a coffee pot. It is removed from the mould after drying and over here we can see handles and spouts being fixed on pots with slip. Next I'd like to show you a process used to produce flat objects such as plates and saucers …

The next step is to clean and smooth the joints of the item after drying overnight. Now we move on to the first firing in this kiln here. This is followed by perhaps the most interesting stage – decorating and glazing, followed by the final firing. There are various methods used in the decoration process, but today I'd like to show you engraving and hand-painting. If you'd like to come this way, we'll have a look at the engraving process used to decorate Spode's famous blue pottery ... Notice here the gold edging being hand-painted onto these plates. It is interesting to note that this gold will withstand dishwashers if treated with reasonable care.

Well, that concludes our tour. I hope you enjoyed it and thank you for coming. You are very welcome to spend some time looking around our museum and factory shop.

Specialist Vocabulary

pottery: Töpferware; Töpferei; *fired and glazed:* gebrannt und glasiert; *9-acre site:* Gelände, Standort mit einer Fläche von 9 Acre (1 Acre entspricht etwa 4047 qm); *underglaze blue printing:* Unterglasurblaudruck; *clay:* Ton(erde); *sieve:* Sieb; *slab:* dicke Scheibe; *pug-mill:* Mischmühle; *to cast:* gießen, formen; *holloware:* Hohlgeschirr; *clay slip:* geschlämmter Ton; *mould:* Guss-, Gießform; *spout:* Tülle; *joints:* Verbindungsstellen; *kiln:* Brenn-, Trockenofen; *to engrave:* gravieren; *to withstand:* standhalten, aushalten.

15. Telephoning Including Making Arrangements

Making international calls can be a difficult business. In a telephone conversation there are no facial expressions, gestures or body language to help you understand the other person. Accents can be a problem, and native speakers may simply take over the conversation. You may also be under time pressure. It helps if you know the special words and phrases you need for making business calls and some of the strategies described below can be useful.

Useful Phrases

First contact

Good morning. / Good afternoon.
I'm calling from France / LGH Ltd / the Milan branch.
This is Jim Smith from GHG in Paris.
This is John Stevens from CBC in London. I'm in the sales department and I'm calling about …

> **Tips**
> - Make sure that you pronounce your name clearly and can spell it if necessary.
> - Notice that you say *This is Jane Bradley*, not **Here is Jane Bradley*.

Finding your correspondent

Can I speak to Mr Chambers, please?
Could you put me through to Mr Chambers, please?

I'd like to speak to Mr Chambers, please.
I'd like to speak to the person in charge of the ABC Project / the sales manager, please.

Identifying yourself (when answering a call)

This is Jim Smith (speaking).
Jim Smith speaking.
Speaking.

Identifying the caller

Who's calling, please?
Could you give me your name, please?

Giving reason for call

I'm calling about …
I'm calling to ask if you can check if … / check that … /
    confirm that …
The reason I'm calling is to …
I'm returning your call.
I'm calling in reply to your fax.
May I ask what it's about? (**asking** for reason for call)

Asking caller to wait and connecting to another speaker

Would you hold on, please?
Just a moment, please.
I'll put you through. / I'll put Ms Baines on. / I'll connect
    you.

The other speaker is not available

Question	Response
I'm sorry, the line's engaged/busy. Would you like to hold? I'm sorry, she's on another line. Will you hold?	Yes, I will. / No, it's alright. I'll call back later.
Would you like to speak to someone else?	Yes, please, if possible. / No, it's okay. I'll try again later.
Mr Hill isn't in his office. Would you like to call back later? Could you call back later, please? Can Mr Lewis call you back?	Yes, I will. / Well, I'm afraid it's rather urgent. Yes, of course. / Well, it's rather important. Is there someone else I could speak to?
Would you like to leave a message?	Yes. Could you ask John to ... / No, it's alright. I'll call back later.

Explaining absences

I'm afraid she's not available at the moment.
I'm afraid he's in a meeting / off sick / on holiday / not in his office at the moment / away on business this week.
I'm afraid she won't be back till Monday.

Taking a message

Can I take a message?
Would you like to leave a message?

Can I give her a message?
I'll give him the message. / I'll pass on the message.

Leaving a message

Could you take a message, please?
Can I leave a message, please?
Could you tell Mr Smith that ... / Could you ask Mr Smith to ...

Promising to do something

I'll tell him you called.
I'll confirm that by email.
I'll get back to you on that.

> **Tips**
> • When talking about action promised for the future, use *I'll ...*, not *I ...*
> • *I'll get back to you on that* means *I'll find out and call you back.*

Problems

I think you've / I've got the wrong number.
Could you speak up, please? It's a bad line.
Could you speak more slowly, please?
I didn't get that. Could you repeat it, please? (For a number or detail)
I didn't catch that. Could you go over it again, please? (For an explanation)

Transferring information

(1) Spelling

Could you spell that, please?
I'll spell that for you.
His name's Wiegand. That's W-I-E-G-A-N-D.

> **Tips**
> - Spelling is easier if you use the table in the appendix which groups letters according to sound (e.g. A, H, J, K are all in the same group) to help you learn the alphabet.
> - Two international spelling systems are also given in the appendix. When using one to spell a word you should say *That's "I" as in India, "G" as in Golf* etc.

(2) Telephone numbers

Each digit in a number is spoken separately. 316740 – *three one six seven four oh.*
0 is *oh* or *zero*.
A double digit – 455621 is pronounced double five. 455621 – *four double five six two one.* 6777832 – *six seven double seven eight three two.*
The number for a country is the *country* or *international code*, and for a city or region the *area code*.

(3) Starting (preparing the other person to receive information)

A: Ready?   B: Yes, go ahead.
A: Can I start? B: (No). Could you just hang on / wait a second, please?

(4) Checking

Can I just read that back to you? (Have **I** got it right?)
Could you just read that back to me? (Have **you** got it
  right?)

(5) Repeating details / confirming

So, that's Monday 14 July at 10.30.
Could you confirm that by fax / in writing, please?
Shall I confirm that by fax/email?

Finishing call

Right./Okay./Fine.
Well, I think that's all.
Is there anything else?

Thank you for your help.
Thank you for calling.

Talk to you soon.
It was nice talking to you.
Goodbye, then. / Bye, then.

> **Tips**
> • The words *right/okay/fine* indicate that a caller
>   wishes to end the call. The next phrases are a polite
>   way of closing the call.
> • You can add other phrases if a future contact is
>   planned e.g. *See you in London next month. / I'll be
>   in touch next week. / Give my regards to Peter.*

Special tips for telephoning
• It is vital to ensure that you have got the message (or
  are getting your message across). Do not hesitate to in-

terrupt as soon as something is not clear. You can stop the conversation by saying *Excuse me* and then using a phrase like *I didn't get that. Could you go over it again, please?* (see above under **Problems**). Even words like *Sorry?/Pardon?* indicate that you are having problems keeping up. You can also repeat key information like *Friday at 6 pm / Monday 23rd / 230 units* etc. to check if you have understood correctly (see above under **Transferring information**).

- It is also important to show that you are following the conversation by using phrases like *I see / Right.* (See above Chapter 7.)
- Lack of facial expression and body language means that you have to convey emotions and attitudes using appropriate language. Be sympathetic if you receive negative news – including complaints. Use phrases like *I understand how you feel. / That must be a problem for you* etc.
- If you have to give negative news, start by using a phrase like *Unfortunately, we have a bit of a problem. / I'm afraid something has come up.*

Conversation (1)

Secretary:	Good morning. GHG Ltd. How can I help you?
Ms Wilson:	Good morning. I'm calling from the Glasgow office. Could I speak to Mr Sims, please?
Secretary:	Could you give me your name, please?
Ms Wilson:	Of course. It's Margaret Wilson.
Secretary:	May I ask what it's about Ms Wilson?
Ms Wilson:	It's about the departmental meeting next month.

Secretary:	Would you hold on, Ms Wilson.
	Pause
	I'm afraid he's not in his office at the moment. Can I give him a message?
Ms Wilson:	Yes, please. Could you tell him that Mr Feldgen from the Munich office won't be able to attend the meeting next week.
Secretary:	Sorry, I didn't catch the name. Could you spell it, please?
Ms Wilson:	Yes. It's Feldgen. That's F-E-L-D-G-E-N.
Secretary:	That's fine, Ms Wilson. I'll pass on the message.
Ms Wilson:	Thank you very much.
Secretary:	You're welcome. Bye.

Conversation (2)

Ms Jackson:	Good morning. Greens Ltd.
Ms Fritsche:	Good morning. This is Ms Fritsche from Berlin. I'd like to speak to Mr Gregg's secretary, please.
Ms Jackson:	This is Sue Jackson speaking. Hi! How are you?
Ms Fritsche:	I'm fine, thanks. And you?
Ms Jackson:	Not too bad. What can I do for you?
Ms Fritsche:	The reason I'm calling is to confirm the details of Herr Walter's visit next month.
Ms Jackson:	Okay. Just let me get the diary. Right.
Ms Fritsche:	So, he'll be arriving on Monday 1st March. He's flying to Heathrow and is due to arrive at 13.20.
Ms Jackson:	Fine. Can you give me his flight number, just in case?

Ms Fritsche:	Of course. It's LH 3204.
Ms Jackson:	So, that's Monday 1st March at 3.20 pm on flight LH 3204.
Ms Fritsche:	Sorry, the time is 13.20. So that's 1.20 pm.
Ms Jackson:	Right. I'll have to get used to the 24-hour clock! Still, I think we've sorted it out now.
Ms Fritsche:	Shall I confirm that by fax or email?
Ms Jackson:	No, it's alright, thanks. We'll send a driver to pick him up, of course.
Ms Fritsche:	That's good, thanks.
Ms Jackson:	You're welcome. So, was there anything else?
Ms Fritsche:	No, that's it for the moment. Thanks once again. Talk to you soon.
Ms Jackson:	Yes. Thanks for calling. Bye.

Making arrangements by phone

Useful phrases

You can **fix** or **arrange** a meeting or an appointment.

You can **cancel** a meeting / an appointment.

Useful sentences

I'm calling to fix a meeting for next Monday.

I'm afraid we will have to cancel next week's meeting. We'll be in touch about another date.

You can **postpone** / **put off** a meeting / an appointment.	Mr Wilcox is off work this week, so can we postpone the meeting until July?
You make a note of appointments in your **diary**.	Let me just get my diary. / I'll just have a look in my diary.

Arranging a meeting/appointment

Reason for calling

I'm calling to fix/arrange a meeting to talk about ... / to discuss ...

Fixing a time and date

When are you free?
When would suit you?
When would be convenient?

How about Thursday 6th October?
How does Thursday 6th October look?
Would Thursday 6th October suit you / be convenient?
Shall we say 3.00 pm?

Saying "yes" / Saying "no"

That would be fine. / I'm afraid I'm busy on 6th.
That's fine. / I'm afraid I'm tied up then.
Yes, I can make/manage 6th. / I'm afraid I can't make/manage 6th.

> **Tips**
> - *I'm tied up* means *I'm busy.*
> - *I can't make/manage 6th* means *I'm busy on 6th.*

• *suit* means *be convenient and cause the least difficulty*. It is pronounced /su:t/.

Confirming details and finishing the call

Right. So, that's Thursday 6th October at 3.00 pm.
I'll look forward to seeing you then.
Mr Black will see you then.
See you then.

Conversation (3)

Pete: Good morning. Pete Turnbull speaking.

Jenny: Hi, Pete. It's Jenny here. The reason I'm calling is to fix a date for our next project meeting.

Pete: Right. I'll just get my diary. So, when are you free? How about Friday 7th June?

Jenny: Might be okay. Depends on the time.

Pete: I could make any time after 2.00 pm.

Jenny: Oh, I'm afraid I'm busy all afternoon.

Pete: Okay. How does Monday 10th look, then?

Jenny: That's better. Would 10.00 am suit you?

Pete: Can we make it 10.30? I've got an appointment at 9.00 and it'll take about an hour.

Jenny: Fine. No problem. So, that's Monday 10th June at 10.30. And I'll arrange a room and let everyone have the details.

Pete: Great! Thanks, Jenny. See you then.

16. Writing Letters, Faxes and Emails

Business correspondence may be very formal (directed to a company or someone you do not know) or less formal (directed to a person you know quite well or even a friend you work with). This aspect is actually more important than whether your communication is a letter, fax or an email. In general, communications have become less formal than they used to be. This is taken into account in the following phrases and tips.

> **Special tips for business communications**
> Keep your sentences short and simple / **K**eep **i**t **s**hort and **s**imple (KISS principle).
> Try to express one idea per paragraph.
> Do not hesitate to use the standard phrases (see below). They express intentions, requests etc. politely and correctly.

A. Letters

There are no longer formal rules for the layout of letters. However, the following example is common today.

Example 1

_____ **XYZ Systems** _____
(Head Office), 7 Bridgeway, Northtown, NO5 3JL
Tel: 061 376890   Fax: 061 376891

Mr T. Spencer   Your ref: Enq. B635
14 Westwell Road   Our ref: DE/476
Swifton
SW3 2SH

4 May 2007   4 May 2007
                                 (alternative position for date)

Dear Mr Spencer

Thank you for your enquiry of 25 April. We are sending you the price list you requested, and would be delighted to hear from you.

Please do not hesitate to get in touch if we can be of
any further help.

Yours sincerely

p.p.

D. Evans
Assistant Sales Manager

Encl. Trade price list

Tips

- The above layout with very little punctuation is now common.
- The recipient's address is on the left and the references and date on the right. However, the date and references may also be on the left above or below the address.
- The sender's address is either in the letterhead (see above), or in the top right-hand corner.
- The paragraphs start at the left margin and there is a line space between them.
- There is no comma after the opening greeting or the closing *Yours sincerely*. In AmE it is common to put commas after both.
- The date is written 4 May (not *the 4th of May or *4. May)
- 6 June 2006 (BrE); June 6, 2006 (AmE)
- The first word after the opening (here: *Thank*) is written with a capital letter.

Opening and closing

BrE	Opening	Closing
Name unknown	Dear Sir/Madam Dear Madam/Sir	Yours faithfully
Name known	Dear Mr/Ms/Miss/ Mrs Smith	Yours sincerely
People you know well	Dear John / Dear Ruth	Best wishes Best/Kind regards

AmE	Opening	Closing
Name unknown	Dear Sir/Madam Dear Madam/Sir	Sincerely (yours) Yours truly

Name known	Dear Mr./Ms./Miss/ Mrs. Smith	Sincerely (yours) Yours truly
People you know well	Dear John / Dear Ruth	Best wishes Best/Kind regards

Tips
- Use the neutral title *Ms* when writing to a woman unless she has used the title *Miss* or *Mrs* herself. (See **Tips,** Chapter 2.)
- Mr, Mrs, Dr etc. are written without full stops in British English, but with full stops in American English. In AmE you use the word *period* for BrE *full stop.*

Stating a reference

Thank you for your letter/fax/email of 12 March.
With reference to our conversation today / your fax of 9 June, …
In answer to your fax of 8 August, …

Saying thank you

I am very grateful to you for sending the catalogue so promptly.
I am very grateful for the information on the conference in December.
Thank you for the documents which we requested.
Thank you for sending the price list.
Thanks for your help.

Note
The above are in decreasing order of formality.

Reason for writing

We are writing to inform you that ... / let you know that ...

I am writing to enquire about ... / ask about ... / let you have the information you wanted.

We are writing to apologize for our delay in delivering your order.

We are writing to apologize for missing the deadline.

We are writing to apologize for not attending to the matter sooner.

I am writing in connection with ... / with regard to ...

I am writing in response to your request for ... / your enquiry about ...

Tips
- Using *I* rather than *we* for the company makes the letter sound less formal.
- It is usual to avoid contractions like *I'm, we're* etc. in formal language.

Main part

Asking for help / information

I/We would be very grateful if you could ...

I would appreciate it if you could ...

Could you please ...?

Giving help/information / good news

You will be pleased to hear that ...

We are pleased to inform you that ...

I am enclosing the documents you requested.

Please find enclosed our latest catalogue.

Bad news

We are sorry to tell you that ...
I am afraid that ...
Unfortunately, ...

Apologizing

I was very concerned to hear about ... / that ...
We were very/extremely sorry to hear about ... / that ...
I am very sorry about the delay in replying.
I apologize for sending you the wrong catalogue.
I would like to apologize for not replying sooner.
Please accept our apologies for any inconvenience this
    has caused you.

Closing remarks

If you have any further questions, please do not hesitate
    to contact/call us.
If I can help in any way, please contact me again / please
    get in touch with me.
Thank you (once again) for your help.
Thank you in advance for your help.

Reference to future contact

I look forward to meeting you / seeing you again / hear-
    ing from you.
Looking forward to meeting you / seeing you again.

> **Tip**
> In the expression *Looking forward to ...*, 'to' is a
> preposition and is followed by the *-ing* form of a verb.
> *I'm looking forward to visiting your factory.*

Useful Abbreviations

- *Your/our ref:* Your/our reference: Ihr/unser Zeichen
- *p.p.*, also *pp* (Latin for 'on behalf of': per pro- curationem) is written before the name of another person when you sign a letter for them: im Auftrage von, i. A.
- *Encl.*, also *enc.:* enclosure (something you send with the letter): Anlage
- *cc/c.c.:* carbon copies, copies to: Kopien an
- *c/o:* care of: (wohnhaft) bei
- *re:* with regard to: in Sachen, betreffs
- *with ref. to:* with reference to: mit Bezug auf

See also section after faxes and emails.

B. Faxes

Faxes are usually less formal than letters, and there is no standard format for faxes. The level of formality depends on the relationship between the sender and recipient. Otherwise the phrases used are similar to those in letters.

Example 2

Fax
_____ **XYZ Systems** _____
(Head Office), 7 Bridgeway, Northtown, NO5 3JL
Tel: 061 376890   Fax: 061 376891

To	ENG Tools
From	David Evans
Date	5 July 2007
Attention	Julie Whitehead
Subject	Order for Loxor 35/BZ
Pages	3 (including this one)

Thanks very much for your order received today. We will deal with it immediately, and you should receive the goods by next week.

If you have any further questions, don't hesitate to get in touch with us. We'll do all we can to be of assistance.

Regards

Tips
- Faxes often include the headings at the beginning of the fax (**To, From** etc.).
- Greetings (Dear Mr Smith etc.) are often omitted in faxes.
- Faxes usually close with *Regards, Best wishes* etc. rather than *Yours sincerely/faithfully*.
- If the fax is not just an informal note, the same formulations as in a letter can be used.

C. Emails

As with other business correspondence, the style of an email depends on the status of the person to whom you are writing. You can use the standard phrases for letter writing in a very formal email. Very informal emails (to people you know well) often use abbreviations and miss out some words and punctuation. This may be a problem for non-native speakers, so it may be better to avoid such a style yourself. The following examples contrast the informal and formal versions of an email.

Example 3 (very informal version)

Subject:	Budget meeting
Date:	3.5.07
From:	bbrown@XYZ.com
To:	cwatts@ABC.org

Hi

How're things?

Next Monday at 9 OK for you? Will arrange room etc. Could u send the final figures asap?

Attached: Suggestions from human resources for cutting costs. Note changes to personnel figures!!! Your opinion??

See you.

Bob

Note

- Informal greeting (*Hi*)
- Use of contraction (*How're* – How are)
- Use of abbreviations (*u* – you; *asap* – as soon as possible)
- Some words are missing (*Next Monday …?* – Is next Monday …?; *Will arrange …* – I will arrange …; *Your opinion?* – What is your opinion?)
- Use of punctuation for emphasis (*Note changes to personnel figures!!!*)

Example 4 (more formal version)

Subject: Budget meeting
Date: 3 May 2007
From: bbrown@XYZ.com
To: cwatts@ABC.org

Dear Mr Watts,

How are you? Well, I hope.

I am writing about the date for our next budget meeting. Would next Monday at 9 suit you? I will arrange for a room and see to the other details.

Could you also send the final figures as soon as possible, please?

I am attaching the suggestions from human resources for cutting costs. Perhaps you could let me know what you think about the proposed changes to the personnel figures.

I look forward to seeing you on Monday.

Best regards

Bob Brown

Abbreviations

The following abbreviations are often found in emails, but it may be best not to use the very colloquial ones to avoid sociocultural misunderstandings.

aob	any other business	*Sonstiges*
asap	as soon as possible	*so schnell wie möglich*
attn	(for the) attention (of)	*zu Händen von*
btw	by the way	*übrigens*
fao	for the attention of	*zu Händen von*
fyi	for your information	*zu Ihrer Information*
pdq	pretty damn quick	*ganz verdammt schnell*
pls	please	*bitte*
rgds	regards	*Grüße*
rtm	read the manual	*lesen Sie das Handbuch*
ta/tx/tnks	thanks	*danke*
tia	thanks in advance	*Dank im Voraus*

Extras (Appendix)

17. Spelling

Spelling can always be rather difficult in any foreign language. Knowing the alphabet is essential. It is helpful to learn the alphabet according to sounds. The following table arranges the alphabet in sound groups, so that you learn which letters sound similar. You can keep a table like this near at hand in case you have to spell a word on the phone, for example.

stay	bee	let	eye	oh	you	are
A	B	F	I	O	Q	R
H	C	L	Y		U	
J	D	M			W	
K	E	N				
	G	S				
	P	X				
	T	Z /zed/				
	V	(BrE)				
	Z /ziː/					
	(AmE)					

International Phonetic Alphabet

Vowels		Consonants	
iː	as in *feet*	j	as in *yes*
ɪ	as in *fit*	w	as in *water*
e	as in *let*	p	as in *pen*
æ	as in *cat*	b	as in *bit*
ɑː	as in *father* and as in *lot* (**GenAmE only**)	t	as in *ten*
		d	as in *done*

Vowels		Consonants	
ɒ	as in *hot* **(BrE only)**	k	as in *can*
ɔː	as in *born*	g	as in *go*
ʊ	as in *put*	tʃ	as in *chair*
uː	as in *pool*	dʒ	as in *gin*
ʌ	as in *cut*	f	as in *four*
ɜː	as in *bird*	v	as in *van*
ə	as in *ago*	θ	as in *thin*
eɪ	as in *name*	ð	as in *than*
əʊ	as in *tone* **(BrE only)**	s	as in *sit*
oʊ	as in *tone* **(GenAmE only)**	z	as in *zone*
		ʃ	as in *shoe*
aɪ	as in *time*	ʒ	as in *genre*
aʊ	as in *town*	h	as in *hen*
ɔɪ	as in *boy*	m	as in *man*
ɪə	as in *fear* **(BrE only)**	n	as in *no*
eə	as in *fair* **(BrE only)**	ŋ	as in *sing*
ʊə	as in *tour* **(BrE only)**	r	as in *red*
		l	as in *lot*

If in doubt, you can also use the **I**nternational **R**adio **Te**legraphy **S**ystem or the **I**nternational **T**elephone **A**lphabet (see below) which both represent an international spelling system.

Letter	Pronun-ciation	IRTS	ITA
A	/eɪ/	**ALPHA** /ˈælfə/	Alfred
B	/biː/	**BRAVO** /ˈbrɑːvəʊ/	Benjamin

Letter	Pronun-ciation	IRTS	ITA
C	/siː/	**CHARLIE** /'tʃɑːlɪ/	Charles
D	/diː/	**DELTA** /'deltə/	David
E	/iː/	**ECHO** /'ekəʊ/	Edward
F	/ef/	**FOXTROT** /'fɒkstrɒt/	Frederick
G	/dʒiː/	**GOLF** /gɒlf/	George
H	/eɪtʃ/	**HOTEL** /həʊ'tel/	Harry
I	/aɪ/	**INDIA** /'ɪndjə/	Isaac
J	/dʒeɪ/	**JULIET** /'dʒuːljet/	Jack
K	/keɪ/	**KILO** /'kiːləʊ/	King
L	/el/	**LIMA** /'liːmə/	London
M	/em/	**MIKE** /maɪk/	Mary
N	/en/	**NOVEMBER** /nəʊ'vembə/	Nellie
O	/əʊ/	**OSCAR** /'ɒskə/	Oliver
P	/piː/	**PAPA** /pə'pɑː/	Peter
Q	/kjuː/	**QUEBEC** /kwɪ'bek/	Queen
R	/ɑː/	**ROMEO** /'rəʊmɪəʊ/	Robert
S	/es/	**SIERRA** /'sjerə/	Samuel
T	/tiː/	**TANGO** /'tæŋgəʊ/	Tommy
U	/juː/	**UNIFORM** /'juːnɪfɔːm/	Uncle
V	/viː/	**VICTOR** /'vɪktə/	Victor
W	/dʌbl juː/	**WHISKY** /'wɪskɪ/	William
X	/eks/	**X-RAY** /'eksreɪ/	X-ray
Y	/waɪ/	**YANKEE** /'jæŋkɪ/	Yellow
Z	/zed/ – /ziː/	**ZULU** /'zuːluː/	Zebra

Conversation

A: I'd like to speak to Madame Allaux, please.

B: I'm sorry, I'm afraid I did not catch the name. Could you spell it, please?

A: Certainly. That's A-L-L-A-U-X.

B: Right. A-L-L-A-U. Madame Allau.

A: No, sorry, A-L-L-A-U-**X** as in "X-RAY".

18. Numbers, Dates and Time

Numbers

Cardinals and Ordinals

Cardinal		Ordinal	
1	one	1st	first
2	two	2nd	second
3	three	3rd	third
4	four	4th	fourth
5	five	5th	fifth
6	six	6th	sixth
7	seven	7th	seventh
8	eight	8th	eighth
9	nine	9th	ninth
10	ten	10th	tenth
11	eleven	11th	eleventh
12	twelve	12th	twelfth
13	thirteen	13th	thirteenth
14	fourteen	14th	fourteenth
15	fifteen	15th	fifteenth
16	sixteen	16th	sixteenth
17	seventeen	17th	seventeenth
18	eighteen	18th	eighteenth
19	nineteen	19th	nineteenth
20	twenty	20th	twentieth
21	twenty-one	21st	twenty-first
22	twenty-two	22nd	twenty-second

Cardinal		Ordinal	
30	thirty	30th	thirtieth
40	forty	40th	fortieth
50	fifty	50th	fiftieth
60	sixty	60th	sixtieth
70	seventy	70th	seventieth
80	eighty	80th	eightieth
90	ninety	90th	ninetieth
100	a hundred	100th	hundredth

Note
Notice the spelling of f**ou**r, f**ou**rteen, f**o**rty.

Large numbers

Written	Spoken
176	a hundred and seventy-six
549	five hundred and forty-nine
1,000	a thousand
2,483	two thousand four hundred and eighty-three
100,000	a hundred thousand
500,627	five hundred thousand six hundred and twenty-seven
1,000,000	a million
1,000,000,000	a billion

Fractions/Decimals

Written	Spoken
¼	a quarter
½	a half
⅓	a third
⅝	five eighths
0.05	nought point oh five
0.5	nought point five
0.34	nought point three four
8.05	eight point oh five
45.45	forty-five point four five

Note

- In English, a comma is used for thousands and millions.
- In English, a full stop or decimal point is used to separate whole numbers from tenths, hundredths etc.
- In British English **0** is pronounced *nought* before a decimal point and *oh* after a decimal point. In American English it can be pronounced *zero*.
- Numbers are pronounced individually after the decimal point.

Dates

Useful sentences

What's today's date?	It's the sixth of July. (6 July)
What's the date today?	It's July the sixth (BrE). It's July sixth (AmE).

Dates	British English	American English
Written	2 October, 2006 2/10/06	October 2, 2006 10/2/06
Spoken	The second of October, 2006 October the second, 2006	October second, 2006

Note

In American English, the month appears before the day in the date abbreviation. Thus, 10/2/98 is October second, 1998.

Years

Written	1983	2007
Spoken	nineteen eighty-three	two thousand and seven

Time

Useful sentences

What's the time?   It's 3 o'clock.
What time is it?
Could you tell me the time, please?

Note

o'clock is only used after the full hour.

Written	Spoken		
Time	Standard I	Standard II	Timetable
15.00	three o'clock	three pm	fifteen hundred (hours)
10.05	five past/after ten	ten oh five am	ten oh five
14.15	a quarter past/after two	two fifteen pm	fourteen fifteen
09.25	twenty-five past/after nine	nine twenty-five am	oh nine twenty-five
21.30	half past/after nine	nine thirty pm	twenty-one thirty
11.45	a quarter to/of twelve	eleven forty-five am	eleven forty-five
23.55	five to/of twelve	eleven fifty-five pm	twenty-three fifty-five

Note
- In American English you can use different prepositions:
  10.05 – five past ten (BrE), five past/after ten (AmE)
  11.45 – a quarter to twelve (BrE), a quarter to/of twelve (AmE) (see Standard I)
- *am* and *pm* are Latin (*ante meridiem, post meridiem*) and designate morning and afternoon.
  am: 12.00 (midnight) to 12.00 (midday)
  pm: 12.00 (midday) to 12.00 (midnight) (see Standard II)

The pronunciation is /eɪ 'em/ (*am*) and /piː 'em/ (*pm*).

- American and British speakers only use the twenty-four hour clock to talk about timetables.

19. An Organigram – A Typical Company Structure

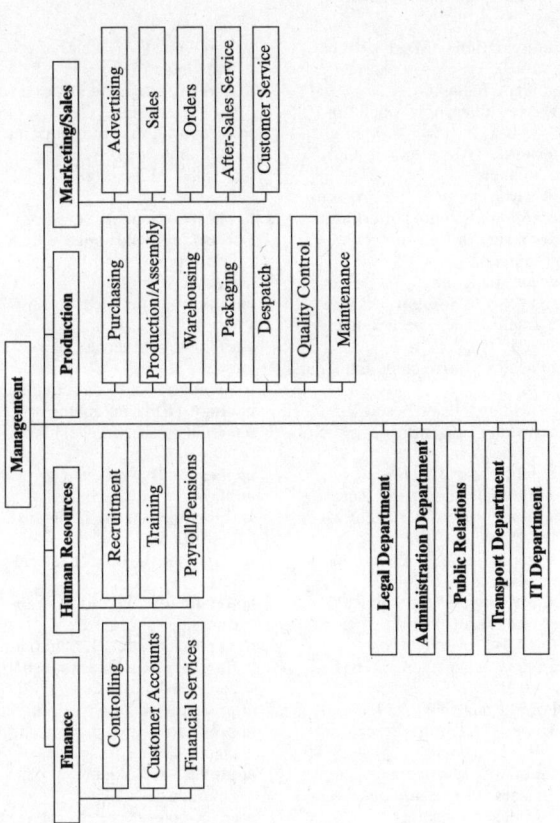

20. Vocabulary

A. English – German

abbreviation (Wort-)Abkürzung

ability Fähigkeit

above über; obig, oben (erwähnt)

absence Abwesenheit, Fernbleiben

accent (sprachlicher) Akzent

accommodation Unterkunft

according to entsprechend, laut, nach

account Konto

to take into **account** in Betracht ziehen, berücksichtigen

to **achieve** erreichen; Erfolg erzielen

to **acknowledge** bestätigen

actual(ly) eigentlich, wirklich, tatsächlich

to **add** hinzufügen

additional zusätzlich, Zusatz ...

adjourn (sich) vertagen; verschieben

administration Verwaltung

in **advance** im Voraus

advertising Werbung, Reklame

advice Rat(schlag)

to **advise** raten

affairs Angelegenheiten; Ereignisse

I am / I'm **afraid** leider

agency Agentur, Geschäftsstelle, Vertretung

agenda Tagesordnung

for **ages** (pl.) seit einer Ewigkeit, seit langem

to **agree on sth.** sich über etwas einigen

to **agree to sth.** mit etwas einverstanden sein

to **agree with sb.** mit jdm. einer Meinung sein

aids (pl.) Hilfsmittel

aim Ziel

to **allow** erlauben, gewähren

(jobseeker's) **allowance** Arbeitslosengeld

a.m./am vormittags

amazing erstaunlich, verblüffend

ambitious ehrgeizig

annual jährlich

to **apologize** sich entschuldigen

apology Entschuldigung

appendix (schriftlicher) Anhang

applicant Bewerber(in)

application Bewerbung

to **apply for sth.** sich um etwas bewerben

to **apply to sth.** für etwas gelten

appointment Termin, Verabredung

to **appreciate sth.** 1. dankbar für etwas sein; 2. etwas schätzen, würdigen

apprenticeship Lehre, Lehrzeit

appropriate angemessen, geeignet

approval 1. Billigung; 2. Anerkennung

area Gebiet, Bereich

area code Vorwahl(nummer)

asking price Angebotspreis

assembly Montage

to be **of assistance to sb.** jdm. behilflich sein

to **attach** beifügen, anhängen

to **attend sth.** an etwas teilnehmen, etwas besuchen

to **attend to sth.** sich um etwas kümmern

attention Beachtung, Aufmerksamkeit

for the **attention** of zu Händen von

attitude Haltung, Einstellung

to **attract sb.'s attention** jds. Aufmerksamkeit auf sich ziehen

audience Zuhörerschaft, Publikum

auxiliary verb Hilfsverb

available verfügbar, vorhanden

awful furchtbar

awkward 1. unbeholfen; 2. peinlich

axis Achse

bankruptcy Bankrott, Konkurs

bar chart Säulen-, Balkendiagramm

to **bargain** handeln, verhandeln, feilschen

based ansässig, mit Sitz

on **behalf of** im Namen, Auftrag von

below unten

social **benefits** (pl.) Sozialhilfe

I had / I'd **better** ich sollte lieber

beyond jenseits, über … hinaus

bill Rechnung

billion Milliarde

blue-collar worker Arbeiter(in)

board 1. Aufsichtsrat, Vorstand; 2. Wandtafel

to get **bogged down** steckenbleiben, sich verzetteln

branch Filiale

break Pause

to **break off** abbrechen, beenden

brief kurz

to **brief sb.** jdn. instruieren

to **bring sb. in** jdn. hinzuziehen, einschalten

bumpy holprig; unruhig (Flug)

to **cancel** absagen, streichen

cardinal Kardinal-, Grundzahl

care Sorgfalt; Pflege

to take **care** aufpassen

in **case** falls

just in **case** für alle Fälle

casual zwanglos, ungezwungen

CEO (chief executive officer) Geschäftsführende(r) Direktor(in)

to **chair** den Vorsitz haben, führen

to be in **charge of sth.** verantwortlich für etwas sein

chart Diagramm, Schaubild

to **check** überprüfen

chess Schach

chief executive Hauptgeschäftsführer(in)

choice (Aus-)Wahl

circuit Stromkreis

to **circulate** in Umlauf bringen; zirkulieren; herumgehen lassen

civil engineer Bauingenieur(in)

clarification Klarstellung

clause Klausel
client Kunde, Kundin; Auftraggeber(in)
to **close a sale** einen Verkauf, ein Geschäft abschließen
colloquial umgangssprachlich
column Spalte
to **come up** anfallen, sich ergeben
commission Provision
common alltäglich; allgemein bekannt
to **compare** vergleichen
competition Konkurrenz, Wettbewerb
competitive wettbewerbsfähig
competitor Konkurrent(in), Mitbewerber(in)
complaint Beschwerde
completely völlig
comprehensive school Gesamtschule
concept Begriff, Vorstellung, Idee
concerned besorgt, betroffen
concession Zugeständnis
to **conclude** beenden, (ab)schließen
confidence Vertrauen
to **confirm** bestätigen
to **confuse** verwechseln
to **connect** verbinden
connection Zusammenhang; Verbindung
to **consider** in Betracht ziehen
to **consist of sth.** aus etwas bestehen
construction business Baubranche, Baugeschäft
content(s) Inhalt
context Zusammenhang
contraction Kurzform

to **contribute** beitragen, beisteuern
contribution Diskussionsbeitrag
convenient passend, günstig
to **convey** vermitteln, übermitteln
to **co-operate/cooperate** zusammenarbeiten
to **cope with sth.** mit etwas fertig werden, zurechtkommen, klarkommen
corporation/corp. Unternehmen
(business) **correspondent** Geschäfts-, Ansprechpartner(in)
costly kostspielig
counter-proposal Gegenvorschlag
to **cover** behandeln, abdecken
criticism Kritik
crucial entscheidend
current aktuell, laufend
currently augenblicklich
customer Kunde, Kundin
to **cut** (costs, jobs, pensions) kürzen, reduzieren

damn (adv.) verflucht, sehr
data-processing Datenverarbeitung
data-storage Datenspeicherung
deadline Stichtag, (Ablieferungs-)Termin
to **deal with sth.** sich mit etwas befassen; etwas erledigen
debts Schulden
to **decline** (höflich) ablehnen
decrease Verringerung, Abnahme
definite bestimmt
degree Hochschulabschluss, akademischer Grad

delay Verzögerung, Verspätung

to be **delayed** sich verspäten

delegate Delegierte(r); Vertreter(in), Beauftragte(r)

delighted erfreut, entzückt

to **deliver** ausliefern

delivery Lieferung, Auslieferung

department Abteilung

to **depend on sth.** von etwas abhängen

it **depends** es kommt darauf an

design Entwurf

to **design** entwerfen

to **designate** festlegen, bestimmen

despatch Versand

diary Terminkalender

to **differ** sich unterscheiden

digit Ziffer, Stelle

digital projector Beamer

to **disagree** anderer Meinung sein, nicht übereinstimmen

disease Krankheit

to **dismiss** entlassen

to be on **display** ausgestellt sein

dissatisfied unzufrieden

distinction Unterscheidung

division Abteilung, Gruppe

domestic 1. inländisch; 2. Haushalts…

to **drop the price** den Preis senken

due to wegen

to be **due to do sth.** etwas tun sollen

to feel at **ease** sich wohl fühlen

efforts Bemühungen

e.g. z. B.

to **employ** beschäftigen

employee Arbeitnehmer(in); Angestellte(r)

employer Arbeitgeber(in)

employment Beschäftigung, Arbeit

to **enable** 1. befähigen; 2. möglich machen

enclosure/encl. Anlage (Brief)

engaged besetzt (Telefon)

engagement Verpflichtung, Verabredung, Termin

engineering company Maschinenbaufirma

to **enquire** (sich) erkundigen

enquiry Anfrage, Nachfrage

to **ensure** dafür sorgen, dass; sicherstellen

enterprise Unternehmen

to **entertain** (Gäste zum Essen) einladen, bewirten

equipment Ausstattung; Gerät, Maschine

to be **equivalent to sth.** einer Sache entsprechen

essential wesentlich, grundlegend

estate agent Immobilienmakler(in)

except außer

exceptional außergewöhnlich

exchange Austausch

exclusivity (clause) Ausschließlichkeit(sklausel)

executive leitende(r) Angestellte(r)

exhibition Ausstellung

to **expand** expandieren, erweitern

to meet sb.'s **expectation** jds. Erwartung entsprechen

to **extend** erweitern, ausweiten

extension Apparat, Telefonnebenanschluss

to some **extent** bis zu einem gewissen Grade

to keep an **eye on sth.** etwas im Auge behalten

to be **faced with sth.** mit etwas konfrontiert sein

face value Nominalwert

facial expression Gesichtsausdruck, Mimik

to **fail** fehlschlagen

fair Messe, Ausstellung

fairly 1. ziemlich; 2. gerechterweise

familiar vertraut, bekannt

to be in **favour** dafür sein, stimmen

feasibility Machbarkeit, Durchführbarkeit

feasible durchführbar, machbar, möglich

figure 1. Zahl; 2. Diagramm, Zeichnung

to **file for bankruptcy** Konkurs anmelden

to **fill sb. in on sth.** jdn. über etwas informieren, ins Bild setzen

finally schließlich

firm Firma

to **fit** passen

to **fix** festmachen, -setzen, vereinbaren

flow chart Flussdiagramm

forecast Voraussage, Vorhersage

forward-looking vorausschauend

fraction Bruch (Mathematik)

freelance freiberuflich; Freiberufler(in); freie(r) Mitarbeiter(in)

in **front of** vor

further weiter(e, s), sonstig; weiter(hin)

go ahead nur zu, bitte schön, natürlich

go-ahead Zustimmung, grünes Licht

goods Güter, Waren

grammar school Gymnasium

graph grafische Darstellung

grateful dankbar

guidelines Richtlinien

gym/gymnasium Turn-, Sporthalle, Fitnessstudio

to **hand over to sb.** jdm. (das Wort) übergeben; jdm. (etwas) überreichen

to **happen** passieren

heading Überschrift, Titelzeile

to **hesitate** zögern

hint Fingerzeig, Tipp

to **hold on** am (Telefon-)Apparat bleiben

holding company Holding-, Dachgesellschaft

host Gastgeber(in)

humid feucht

to **identify a problem** ein Problem erkennen

i.e. das heißt

to **improve** (sich) bessern; verbessern

to **include** einschließen, beinhalten

inconvenience Unannehmlichkeit(en)

to **increase** erhöhen

indefinite unbestimmt

to **indicate** 1. be-, andeuten; 2. angeben, bezeichnen; 3. zeigen

informal informell, umgangssprachlich
to **insist** (darauf) bestehen
for **instance** zum Beispiel
invention Entdeckung
to **involve** einbeziehen; erfordern; bedeuten
issue Frage, Problem, Thema
item Punkt, Posten, Artikel,
Gegenstand

traffic **jam** Verkehrsstau
to **join sb.** sich jdm. anschließen
to **join sth.** in etwas eintreten,
zu etwas gehen
joint venture Gemeinschafts-
projekt; Arbeits-, Projektge-
meinschaft; Beteiligungsge-
schäft

to **keep an eye on sth.** etwas
im Auge behalten
to **keep to the point** bei der Sache bleiben, sich auf das We-
sentliche konzentrieren

lack Mangel, Fehlen
least wenigste(r, s), gerings-
te(r, s)
to **leave sth. to sb.** jdm. etwas
überlassen
leisure Freizeit, freie Zeit
letterhead Briefkopf
liability Haftung
to give sb. a **lift** jdn. im Auto
mitnehmen
likely wahrscheinlich, voraus-
sichtlich
likewise desgleichen, ebenso
line manager 1. Produktlinien-
manager(in); 2. unmittelba-
re(r) Vorgesetzte(r); 3. Fach-
gebietsleiter(in)

line space Leerzeile
to **list** auflisten
to **look forward to sth.** sich auf
etwas freuen, auf etwas hoffen
Ltd GmbH

maintenance Wartung
major bedeutend, wichtig
I can **make it** ich kann es
schaffen, arrangieren
managing director (MD) Ge-
schäftsführer(in)
to **manufacture** herstellen, er-
zeugen
margin (Seiten-)Rand
marital status Familienstand
(*marital:* ehelich)
marker pen Marker, Markier-
stift
matter Angelegenheit
it does not / doesn't **matter**
es macht nichts
to **mean** bedeuten
merger (Firmen-)Fusion
to get one's **message**
across sich verständlich machen
to **mind sth.** etwas gegen eine
Sache haben
minor geringfügig, kleiner(e, s)
minutes (pl.) (Sitzungs-)Proto-
koll
to take the **minutes** Protokoll
führen
misgivings Zweifel, Befürch-
tungen, Bedenken
to **miss** 1. auslassen; 2. verpas-
sen; 3. nicht mitbekommen
mobile (phone) Handy
to **monitor** überwachen, (prü-
fend) verfolgen, überprüfen
multinational Multi, multina-
tionaler Konzern

to **negotiate**   verhandeln

to set up **negotiations**   Verhandlungen vorbereiten, aufnehmen, einleiten

to be **non-committal**   unverbindlich sein, sich nicht festlegen wollen

occasionally   gelegentlich

to **occur**   sich ereignen, vorkommen

I am / I'm **off**   ich muss los, gehen

off work   krankgeschrieben

to **omit**   auslassen, weglassen

opposite   1. gegenüberliegend; **2.** Gegenteil

order   1. Bestellung; **2.** Auftrag; **3.** Reihenfolge

ordinal   Ordnungszahl

otherwise   sonst, ansonsten

to **outline sth.**   einen Überblick über etwas geben

outright (adv.)   ohne Umschweife, auf der Stelle, sofort

to **outsource**   (Aufträge) nach außen vergeben

outstanding   unerledigt, ausstehend

overhead   Overheadfolie

panel   Diskussionsrunde, -team, -teilnehmer(innen)

parcel   Paket, Päckchen

pardon   wie bitte?

parent company   Muttergesellschaft (*parent*: Elternteil)

participant   Teilnehmer(in)

in **particular**   vor allem, insbesondere

particularly   besonders, speziell

to **pass sth. on**   etwas weitergeben, -leiten

past   1. nach; **2.** Vergangenheit

pattern   Schema, Muster

payroll   Lohn-, Gehaltsliste

per   durch, pro, je

performance   Leistung

personnel   Personal, Belegschaft

to **pick sb. up**   jdn. abholen

pie chart   Kreisdiagramm

to **pinpoint sth.**   die Aufmerksamkeit auf etwas lenken, etwas herausstellen, hervorheben

to **place**   platzieren, setzen

plane   Flugzeug

plant   Betrieb, Werk

plc (public limited company)   AG

plug   Stecker, Steckdose

p.m./pm   nachmittags

pointer   Pointer, Zeigestock

to **point out sth.**   aufmerksam auf etwas machen

to **point to sth.**   auf etwas zeigen

to **pop into**   vorbeischauen, kurz hineingehen

to **postpone**   verschieben, aufschieben

preliminary   Vor..., vorbereitend, einleitend

premises   Räumlichkeiten, (Geschäfts-)Räume

pressure   Druck

primary school   Grundschule

small **print**   Kleingedrucktes

priority   Priorität, Vorrang

progress   Fortschritt(e)

properly   richtig

property   1. Grundstück; **2.** Besitz

proposal   Vorschlag

prospective   potenziell

to **provide** bereitstellen; versorgen

public öffentlich; Öffentlichkeit

to **publish** publizieren, veröffentlichen

to **purchase** kaufen, erwerben

purpose Zweck, Ziel, Absicht

to **put off** verschieben, aufschieben

to **raise** erhöhen

range Sortiment, Kollektion

rapport (harmonisches) Verhältnis, Beziehung

rate Quote, Rate

I had / I'd **rather** ich würde lieber, mir wäre es lieber

reasonable vernünftig, angemessen, realistisch

recently vor kurzem, in letzter Zeit

recipient Empfänger(in)

to **recommend** empfehlen

record Aufzeichnung, Niederschrift

to **recruit** (neu) einstellen, Neueinstellung(en) vornehmen

recruitment Neueinstellung; Personalbeschaffung

redundancy Entlassung, (betriebsbedingte) Freistellung

redundant arbeitslos

to **refer to sth.** auf etwas verweisen, sich auf etwas beziehen

reference Bezug, Verweis

with **regard to** bezüglich, in Bezug auf

regardless of ungeachtet, ohne Rücksicht auf

to **reject** ablehnen

relation Beziehung

relationship Verhältnis, Beziehung

remaining verbleibend, restlich

to **rephrase a question** eine Frage umformulieren, anders ausdrücken

to **report to sb. 1.** an jdn. berichten; **2.** jdm. unterstellt sein

rep(resentative) Vertreter(in)

request Bitte, Wunsch

to **request sth.** um etwas bitten

to **require** erfordern, verlangen

to **reschedule** neu festlegen, verschieben

research Forschung

to **resign** Amt niederlegen, zurücktreten

human **resources** (pl.) Arbeitskräftepotenzial; Personalabteilung

respectively respektive, beziehungsweise

in **response to** als Antwort auf

to **resume** wieder aufnehmen, fortsetzen

retirement Ruhestand, Pensionierung

to take early **retirement** vorzeitig in Rente gehen

to **return a call** einen Telefonanruf erwidern

rule Regel

rush Eile

rusty eingerostet, rostig

to **sack** entlassen

salary Gehalt

sales manager Verkaufs-, Vertriebsleiter(in)

sales rep(resentative) Handelsvertreter(in)

savings Einsparungen

schedule Zeit-, Arbeitsplan, Programm
to be on schedule planmäßig ablaufen
scientific wissenschaftlich
scope Rahmen, Umfang, Ausmaß
secondary school weiterführende Schule; Realschule
self-employed selbständig, freiberuflich (tätig)
to set up a business ein Geschäft, eine Firma gründen
to settle in sich eingewöhnen
share(s) (Geschäfts-, Markt-)Anteil(e); Aktie(n)
shareholder Aktionär(in), Gesellschafter(in)
skill Fertigkeit
slide Dia
SMEs (small and medium-sized enterprises) mittelständische Betriebe; Mittelstand
socket Steckdose, Anschluss
to soften (ab)mildern, dämpfen
solid 1. fest; 2. ununterbrochen, zusammenhängend (Linie)
to sort sth. / sort out sth. etwas klären, lösen
source Quelle, Ursprung
specifications genaue Angaben
staff Personal, Belegschaft
stage 1. Stadium, Phase; 2. Schritt
stalemate Patt(situation)
stock exchange/market Börse
storage Speicherung; Lagerung
straight on geradeaus
to get stuck steckenbleiben
subject 1. Thema, Anlass; 2. Fach(gebiet)

subsequent nachfolgend, später
subsidiary Tochtergesellschaft
to subsidize subventionieren
subsidy Subvention
to suggest vorschlagen
suitable geeignet, passend
to sum up (abschließend) zusammenfassen
to summarize zusammenfassen, resümieren
superior Vorgesetzte(r), Chef(in)
supplier Lieferant(in)
suppose/supposing vorausgesetzt; angenommen, dass
surprise Überraschung
survey 1. Gutachten; 2. Begutachtung (eines Gebäudes)
surveyor Gutachter(in) (eines Gebäudes), Sachverständige(r)
syllable Silbe
sympathetic verständnisvoll, mitfühlend
sympathy Verständnis, Mitgefühl

table Tabelle
tag (Frage-)Anhängsel
take care! mach's, machen Sie's gut!
to take part in sth. an etwas teilnehmen
takeover Übernahme
taxes Steuern
teething troubles Anlaufschwierigkeiten, Kinderkrankheiten
tense Zeitform
terms Bedingungen, Konditionen

to get on first-name **terms** sich
mit Vornamen anreden
thus folglich, so, somit
tied up beschäftigt
on **time** rechtzeitig, pünktlich
time-consuming zeitaufwendig
timeout Auszeit
timetable Fahrplan, Zeitplan
tool Werkzeug, Gerät
top oberer Teil, oberes Ende
topic Thema
to be/get in **touch** sich melden,
Kontakt aufnehmen
trade Handel
traffic Verkehr
trainee Auszubildende(r),
Praktikant(in)
to **transfer** übermitteln
transparency Overheadfolie
turnover Umsatz

UK (United Kingdom) Verei-
nigtes Königreich
unacceptable unannehmbar,
unzumutbar
to **underline** unterstreichen
unemployment Arbeitslosigkeit
trade **union** Gewerkschaft
unit Stück, Einheit; Lernein-
heit
unless wenn, sofern nicht

urgent dringend
utility Versorgungsbetrieb

value Wert
to **value sth.** etwas bewerten,
den Wert von etwas schätzen
various verschieden, mehrere
to **vary** variieren
venue Tagungsort, Treffpunkt
view Sicht, Ansicht, Meinung
visuals (pl.) Anschauungsmaterial
vital lebenswichtig, äußerst
wichtig, unbedingt nötig
to **vote on sth.** über etwas abstimmen
vowel Vokal

wage Lohn
warehouse Lager(haus)
warehousing Lagerung, Lager-
haltung
(natural) **wastage** natürliche
Fluktuation, Personalreduzierung
whereabouts wo, in welcher
Gegend
whereas während, wohingegen
white-collar worker Angestell-
te(r)
workforce Belegschaft

B. German – English

Bei typischen Wortverbindungen (Kollokationen) finden Sie den Eintrag unter dem Substantiv. Durch *Kursivschrift* werden die verschiedenen Bedeutungen polysemer Wörter, der fachsprachliche Gebrauch und das amerikanische Englisch (*AmE*) gekennzeichnet.

abbrechen to break off
von etwas **abhängen** to depend on sth.
abheben (*vom Konto*) to draw, to withdraw
Abkürzung abbreviation
ablehnen to reject
(höflich) **ablehnen** to decline
Ablieferungstermin, -datum deadline
Abnahme (*Kauf*) purchase
Abnahme (*Verringerung*) decrease
absagen to cancel
Absatz (*Verkauf*) sales
Absicht purpose, intention
abstimmen to vote
Abteilung department, division
Abwesenheit absence
Achse (*mathem.*) axis
Agentur agency
Akte file
Aktie share, stock
Aktiengesellschaft (AG) public limited company (plc)
Aktieninhaber(in) shareholder
aktuell current
Analyse analysis
analysieren to analyse
anbieten to offer
Anfrage enquiry, inquiry
Angebot offer, tender, supply
Angebot machen to tender
Angelegenheit matter, affair

Angestellte(r) white-collar worker
Anlage (*wirtsch.: Beilage*) enclosure
Anlagekapital fixed capital
Anrufbeantworter answerphone, answerer (*AmE*)
ansässig based
Anschauungsmaterial visuals
Anteil share
Antrag application
Anzeige advertisement
Arbeiter(in) (blue-collar) worker
angelernte(r) **Arbeiter(in)** semi-skilled worker
(Fach-)**Arbeiter(in)** skilled worker
ungelernte(r) **Arbeiter(in)** labourer
Arbeitgeber(in) employer
Arbeitnehmer(in) employee
Arbeitsbedingungen working conditions
Arbeitslöhne wages, labour costs
arbeitslos unemployed
Arbeitslosengeld (job seeker's) allowance
Arbeitslosigkeit unemployment
gleitende **Arbeitszeit** flexitime, flextime (*AmE*)
Aufgabe task, job
Aufmerksamkeit auf etwas lenken to pinpoint sth.

Aufschwung rally, recovery

Aufsichtsrat board

Auftrag order

im **Auftrag von** p.p. (per procurationem)

Aufträge nach außen vergeben to outsource

Aufzeichnung (*Niederschrift*) record

ausbilden to train

Ausgaben expenditure, outgoings

ausliefern to deliver

Auslieferung delivery

Außenhandel foreign trade

Außenhandelsdefizit trade gap, trade deficit

Ausstattung (*Geräte, Maschinen*) equipment

ausstehend outstanding

Ausstellung exhibition

ausweiten to extend

Auszubildende(r) trainee

Balkendiagramm bar chart

Bankkredit bank loan

Bargeld cash, hard cash

Bargeldautomat cash dispenser, ATM

Baubranche construction business

Beamer digital projector

etwas **bearbeiten** to deal with sth., to process sth.

Bedarf demand

Bedingung term, condition

beeinträchtigen to affect

befördern (*im Beruf*) to promote

Begutachtung survey

Behörde (public) authority, office, service

beifügen (*anhängen*) to attach

Belegschaft workforce

berechnen (*Geld*) to charge

berechnen (*kalkulieren*) to calculate

bereitstellen to provide

Bericht report

berücksichtigen to take into account

Beruf job, occupation, profession

Beschaffung procurement

beschäftigen to employ

mit etwas **beschäftigt** busy with sth.

Beschäftigung (*Arbeit*) employment

Beschwerde complaint

bestätigen to confirm

bestellen to order

Bestellung order

besteuern to tax

Besteuerung taxation

in **Betracht ziehen** to consider, to take into account

Betrieb company, business, firm

Betriebsgewinn operating profit

Betriebsrat works council

sich um etwas **bewerben** to apply for sth.

Bewerber(in) applicant

Bewerbung application

bewerten (*Wert schätzen*) to value

Beziehung relation, relationship

bezüglich with regard to

Bilanz financial statement, balance

Bilanzaufstellung balance sheet

Binnenmarkt domestic/home market

Börse stock exchange, stock market

Bruttoeinkommen gross income

Bruttoertrag gross return, gross yield

Bruttoinlandseinkommen gross domestic product (GDP)

Bruttosozialprodukt gross national product (GNP)

Buchführung accounting, bookkeeping

Chef(in) boss, superior

Dachgesellschaft holding company

dankbar sein (*schätzen*) to appreciate, to be grateful

Darlehen loan

Datei file

Daten data, facts

Datenverarbeitung data-processing

Delegierte(r) delegate

Devisenkurs exchange rate

Diagramm chart, graph, diagram

Dienstleistungen services

Dienstleistungsgewerbe service industry/industries

dringend urgent

im **Durchschnitt** on average

Eigenkapital capital resources, equity capital

eigentlich actually

Eigentum property

Einfuhrgenehmigung import licence

Einfuhrzoll import duty, customs duty

Eingangssteuersatz basic rate

sich über etwas **einigen** to agree on sth.

einkaufen purchase, shop, buy

Einkäufer(in) buyer, purchasing agent

Einkommen income, earnings

Einkommen(s)steuer (personal) income tax

Einkünfte unearned income

Einnahmen takings, proceeds, earnings

einreichen (*unterbreiten*) to submit, to tender

einschließen im Preis to include in the price

einsparen to save, to economize

Einsparungen savings

einstellen (*Arbeiter usw.*) to take on, to recruit

Einstellung (*von Arbeitskräften*) employment, recruitment

mit etwas **einverstanden sein** to agree to sth.

Einzelhandel retail trade

Einzelhändler(in) retailer

Empfänger(in) (*eines Auftrags*) recipient, receiver

Empfänger(in) (*eines Briefes*) addressee

empfehlen to recommend

Endverbraucher(in) end user, consumer

entlassen to make redundant, to dismiss, to sack, to lay-off

Entlassung redundancy, dismissal, sack, lay-off

Entlassungsabfindung redundancy payment, severance pay

entschädigen to compensate

Entwurf (*Gestaltung*) design

Entwurf (*Konzept*) draft
Erfolg achievement, success
erfordern to require
erhöhen to raise, to increase
erkundigen to enquire, to inquire
etwas **erledigen** (*sich um etwas kümmern*) to deal with sth., to take care of sth.
Ertrag return, yield, profits
erweitern to expand

Fabrik factory, plant
Fähigkeit ability
fallen (*Preise* usw.) to fall, to decrease
Fertigkeit skill
Fertigungsstraße production line
festmachen (*Datum*) to fix
Filiale branch
Firma firm, company
Firmenaufkauf acquisition
Firmenzentrale headquarters
Fließband assembly line
(natürliche) Fluktuation natural wastage
Flussdiagramm flow chart
Forschung research
Fortschritt(e) progress
(*Gespräche*) **fortsetzen** to resume talks
Fracht cargo
Fragebogen questionnaire
Freiberufler(in) freelance
freiberuflich freelance
Führung management
Führungskraft executive
Fusion (*wirtsch.*) merger

Gebühr charge, fee
Gehalt salary
Geldstrafe fine

Genehmigung (*Erlaubnis*) approval, permission, authorization
Genehmigung (*Lizenz*) licence, license (*AmE*), permit
Geschäft abschließen to close a sale
Geschäft gründen to set up a business
Geschäftsführer(in) managing director (MD)
Geschäftsführende(r) Direktor(in) chief executive officer (CEO)
Geschäftsjahr financial year
Geschäftsräume, -gelände premises
Gewerkschaft (trade) union, labor union (*AmE*)
Gewinn profit, gain
Gewinnbeteiligung profit sharing
GmbH Ltd (limited liability company)
Großhandel wholesale
gültig valid
Gutachten (*durch Experten*) expert opinion, report
Gutachten (*eines Gebäudes*) survey
Gutachter(in) (*Experte*) expert
Gutachter(in) (*eines Gebäudes*) surveyor

zu **Händen von** attention of
(unbeschränkte) **Haftung** (unlimited) liability
Handel trade, commerce
handeln (*feilschen*) to bargain
handeln (*wirtsch.*) to trade, to do business
Handelsbilanz balance of trade

Handelsvertreter(in)   sales rep(resentative)

Handy   mobile (phone), cell phone (*AmE*)

Hauptgeschäftsstelle   head office

Haushaltsplan   budget

herstellen   to manufacture, to produce

Hersteller(in)   manufacturer, producer

Herstellung   production

Hochschulabschluss   degree

Holdinggesellschaft   holding company

Honorar   fee

Hypothek   mortgage

verarbeitende **Industrie**   process industry

Ingenieur(in)   engineer

inländisch   domestic

insolvent   bankrupt

Insolvenz   bankruptcy

instruieren   to brief, to inform

Inventur   stocktaking

Inventur machen   to take stock

Investition   investment

jährlich   annual

Jahresbericht   annual report

Jahreshauptversammlung   annual general meeting

potenzielle(r) **Käufer(in)**   prospective buyer

Käufermarkt   buyer's market

Kapitalertragssteuer   capital gains tax

Kauf   purchase, buying

kaufen   to purchase, to buy

etwas **klären** (*lösen*)   to sort sth., to sort out sth.

Klarstellung   clarification

Klausel   clause

Kleingedrucktes   small print

Körperschaftssteuer   corporation tax

Komitee   committee

konfrontiert mit   faced with

Konkurrent(in)   competitor

Konkurrenz   competition

Konkurs   bankruptcy

Konto   bank account, account

Kontoauszug   bank statement

(feste) **Kosten**   fixed costs, expenses

(laufende) **Kosten**   running costs, overheads

Kostennutzenanalyse   cost-benefit analysis

Kostenvoranschlag   estimate

kostspielig   costly

Krankengeld   sickness benefit

Kreisdiagramm   pie chart

Kritik   criticism

sich um etwas **kümmern**   to take care of sth., to deal with sth., to attend to sth.

kündigen (von Mitarbeitern)   to dismiss, to give notice, to make redundant, to sack

Kündigung   dismissal, notice, redundancy, sack

kürzen (*reduzieren*)   to cut

Kunde, Kundin   customer

Kundendienst   (after-sales) service

kurzfristig   short-term

Lager (*Raum*)   stockroom, store

Lagerhaus   warehouse

lagern   to store

Lagerung   storage

Lebenshaltungskosten cost of living

Lebenslauf CV (curriculum vitae), résumé (*AmE*)

lebenswichtig (*unbedingt nötig*) vital

Lehre apprenticeship

leider I am / I'm afraid

Leistung performance

ich würde / es wäre mir **lieber** I had / I'd rather

Lieferant(in) supplier

liefern to deliver, to supply

Lieferung delivery, supplies

Linienflug scheduled flight

Lohn wage

Lohnkosten wage costs, labour costs

Lohnliste payroll

Luftfracht air cargo

Machbarkeit feasibility

Makler(in) (*von Immobilien*) estate agent, real estate agent (*AmE*)

Makler(in) (*an der Börse*) (stock) broker

Mangel an lack, shortage of

Marke (*Industriegüter*) make

Marke (*Lebens- und Genussmittel*) brand

Marktanteil market share

Marktforschung market research

Marktwert market value

(freie) **Marktwirtschaft** free enterprise, free market economy

Mehrwertsteuer VAT (value added tax)

Meinung opinion

anderer **Meinung** sein disagree

Menge quantity, amount

Messe fair

messen measure

Miete rent, rental

mieten to hire, to lease, to rent

Mieter(in) tenant

Milliarde billion

Mitarbeiterstab staff

Mitbewerber(in) competitor

jdm. etwas **mitteilen** to inform, to fill sb. in on s.th., to notify

Mitteilung (*Nachricht*) memo, message, (piece of) information

Mittelstand (*mittelständische Betriebe*) SMEs (small and medium-sized enterprises)

Montage (*Zusammenbau*) assembly

Muster (*Schema*) pattern

Muttergesellschaft parent company

Nachfolger(in) successor

Nachfrage nach demand for

Nachnahme cash on delivery

Nachteil disadvantage

netto net

Nettoeinkommen net income

Nettogewinnspanne net margin

Amt **niederlegen** to resign

Notiz note

null und nichtig null and void

öffentlich public

Öffentlichkeit the public

Overheadfolie transparency, overhead

Pauschalbetrag lump sum

Pensionierung retirement

Pensionskasse pension fund

Personal staff, human resources, personnel

Personalabteilung human resources, personnel department

Personalreduzierung (natural) wastage, staff cuts

Posten (*auf einer Rechnung*) item

Postleitzahl postcode, zip code (*AmE*)

Praktikant(in) trainee

Preisangebot quotation

Presseverlautbarung press release

Produktionsmenge output, batch

Proforma-Rechnung pro forma invoice

Prospekt brochure, folder, prospectus

(Sitzungs-)**Protokoll** minutes

Provision commission

Prozent percent

Prozentsatz percentage

prüfen (*nachprüfen*) to check

pünktlich (*rechtzeitig*) on time

Quelle source

Quittung receipt

Quote rate

Rabatt discount

Rate (*Abzahlung*) instalment

Rechnung (*für Waren*) invoice

Rechnung (*wirtsch.*) bill

Regel rule

Reihenfolge order, sequence

Reklame advertising

Rendite (net) yield, rate of return

Rentabilität profitability

Rente pension, superannuation

restlich remaining

Revision (*wirtsch.*) audit

Richtlinien guidelines

Rücklagen reserves, savings

Ruhestand retirement

Rundschreiben circular (letter)

Säulendiagramm bar chart

Saldo (account) balance

Satz (*Tarif, Preis*) rate

Schadenersatz damages, compensation, indemnity

(einen Wert) **schätzen** to estimate, to value, to assess

Schattenwirtschaft black economy

Schaubild chart, graph, diagram

Schicht (*Arbeitszeit*) shift

Schmiergeld bribe

Schmiergeldfonds slush fund

Schreibarbeit paperwork

Schulden debts

Schuldner(in) debtor

Schwerindustrie heavy industry

senken to lower, to decrease

sicherstellen (*dafür sorgen, dass*) to ensure

sinken to fall, to decrease

Sortiment range

Sozialhilfe benefits

Sozialversicherung social security, national insurance

Sparkonto savings account

Sperrkonto blocked/frozen account

Spesen expenses

Stadium stage

Stammkunde, -kundin regular customer

Standort (*einer Industrie*) site
steigen rise, increase
Steueraufkommen revenue
Steuerfreibetrag tax allowance
Steuerhinterziehung tax evasion
Steuern taxes
Steuerparadies tax haven
steuerpflichtig taxable
Stilllegung shutdown
Straßentransport haulage
Streudiagramm scatter diagram
Stückkosten unit cost
Subunternehmer(in) subcontractor
Subvention subsidy

Tagesordnung agenda
Tagungsort venue
Tantiemen royalties
Tarifvereinbarung wage agreement
Tarifverhandlungen wage negotiations, collective bargaining
Technik (*Technologie*) technology
Technik (*Verfahren*) technique
an etwas teilnehmen to take part in sth.
Teilnehmer(in) participant
Teilzeitarbeiter(in) part-time worker
Telefonnebenanschluss extension
(letzter Ablieferungs-)**Termin** (*Stichtag*) deadline
Termin (*Verabredung*) appointment
Terminkalender diary
Thema (*Inhalt*) subject
Thema (*beim Gespräch*) topic

Thema wechseln to change the subject
Tochtergesellschaft subsidiary
Transportunternehmen haulage contractor

einen **Überblick geben** to outline
übereinstimmen to agree
überfällig overdue
übergeben (*überreichen*) to hand over
jdm. etwas **überlassen** to leave sth. to sb.
Überleben survival
Übernahme takeover
Übernahmeangebot takeover bid
überprüfen to monitor, to check, to verify
Überschuss surplus, profit
Überstunden overtime
überweisen (*Geld*) to transfer, to remit
Überweisung (*Geld*) transfer, remittance
Überziehungskredit overdraft
Umfang (*beim Verkauf*) volume
Umfrage opinion poll, survey
in **Umlauf bringen** to circulate
Umsatz turnover
Umsatzsteuer turnover tax
umschulen to retrain
Umtausch exchange
Umwelt environment
Unterkunft accommodation
Unternehmen enterprise, company
Unternehmensberater(in) management consultant
Unternehmensstrategie corporate strategy

sich **unterscheiden** to differ
Unterscheidung distinction,
difference
unterstreichen to underline
unverbindlich (*Antwort*) non-
committal

für etwas **verantwortlich
sein** to be in charge of sth.,
to be responsible for sth.
verbessern to improve
Verbindung (*Zusammenhang*) connection
Verbrauch consumption
Verbraucher(in) consumer
verfügbar (*vorhanden*) available
vergleichen to compare
verhandeln to negotiate
Verhandlung negotiation
Verkäufer(in) (*jurist.*) seller,
vendor
Verkäufer(in) (*Vertreter*) sales
rep(resentative), salesperson
Verkäufer(in) (*im Laden*)
(shop) assistant, salesclerk
(*AmE*)
Verkauf sale
verkaufen to sell
Verlust loss
vermeiden to avoid
Vermerk note
Vermögenssteuer property tax,
wealth tax
Versand despatch, dispatch
verschieben (*aufschieben*) to
postpone, to put off
verschieben (*Termin neu festlegen*) to reschedule
Versicherungsgesellschaft insurance company
versorgen (*bereitstellen*) to
provide

Versorgungsbetrieb utility
(sich) **vertagen** to adjourn
Vertrag contract, agreement
vertraulich confidential
Vertreter(in) representative,
agent
Vertretung agency, representa-
tion
Vertrieb distribution, sale
Verwaltung administration,
admin
auf etwas **verweisen** to refer to
sth.
Verzögerung delay
vierteljährlich quarterly
Visitenkarte business card
Vollbeschäftigung full employ-
ment
vorausgesetzt suppose, suppos-
ing
Vorgesetzte(r) boss, superior
Vorrang (*Priorität*) priority
Vorrat stock, supplies
vorrätig in stock, available
Vorschlag proposal
vorschlagen to propose, to sug-
gest
Vorschriften regulations, rules
Vorsitz chair
Vorsitzende(r) chairman,
chairwoman, chairperson
Vorstand board
Vorteil advantage
Vorwahl area code

Wachstumsrate growth rate
wählen (*abstimmen*) to vote
Währung currency
Wahl (*Auswahl*) choice
Wahl (*polit.*) election
Wahl (*Vorkaufsrecht*) option
Waren goods
Warenhaus department store

Warenlager stock
Warenmuster sample
Warenrechnung invoice
Wartung maintenance, service
Werbung advertising, advertisement
Werk plant, factory
Werkzeug tool
Wert value
Wertminderung depreciation
wesentlich essential
Wettbewerb competition
Wirkung effect
Wirtschaft economy
(gewerbliche) **Wirtschaft** trade and industry
wirtschaftlich economic
Wohlfahrtsstaat welfare state
Wohlstand prosperity, affluence

Zahl (*Betrag*) figure
Zahlenreihe column
zeitaufwendig time-consuming
Zeitplan schedule, timetable

Ziel aim, purpose, objective, target
Zinsen interest
Zinssatz interest rate
Zoll (customs) duty
Zollerklärung customs declaration
Zollschranke customs barrier
Zugeständnis concession
zurücktreten (*von einem Amt*) to resign
zusammenarbeiten to co-operate/cooperate
zusammenfassen to summarize
Zusammenhang (*Textzusammenhang*) context
Zusammenhang (*Verbindung*) connection
zuständig competent, responsible
zuteilen to allot, to allocate, to assign
zuverlässig reliable, responsible
Zweck purpose

Fremdsprachentexte

IN RECLAMS UNIVERSAL-BIBLIOTHEK

Amerikanische Literatur (Auswahl)

Ernest Hemingway: The Old Man and the Sea. 140 S. UB 9075 – The Snows of Kilimanjaro. Six Stories. 176 S. UB 9120

Patricia Highsmith: A Shot from Nowhere. Six Stories. 160 S. UB 9262 – The Talented Mr. Ripley. 437 S. UB 9145

Denis Johnson: Jesus' Son. 157 S. UB 9092

Kiss Me, Kate. A Musical. (Book Samuel and Bella Spewack, Music and Lyrics Cole Porter) 181 S. UB 9263

Kressmann Taylor: Address Unknown. 63 S. UB 9107

Nick McDonell: Twelve. 237 S. UB 9127

Herman Melville: Bartleby. 88 S. UB 9190

Arthur Miller: Death of a Salesman. 171 S. UB 9172 – The Crucible. 224 S. UB 9257

Mexican-American Short Stories. 179 S. UB 9124

Modern American Short Stories. 160 S. UB 9216

New York Fiction. 154 S. UB 9070

Eugene O'Neill: Long Day's Journey into Night. 216 S. UB 9252

Edgar Allan Poe: The Gold-Bug and Other Tales. 192 S. UB 9173 – The Murders in the Rue Morgue. 80 S. UB 9088

Morton Rhue: Give a Boy a Gun. 195 S. UB 9111

John Steinbeck: Of Mice and Men. 173 S. UB 9253 – Tortilla Flat. 280 S. UB 9027

James Thurber: Stories and Fables of Our Time. Ill. 88 S. UB 9232

West Side Story. A Musical. (Jerome Robbins / Arthur Laurents / Leonard Bernstein / Stephen Sondheim.) 136 S. UB 9212

Thornton Wilder: The Bridge of San Luis Rey. 152 S. UB 9195 – Our Town. 127 S. UB 9168

Tennessee Williams: Cat on a Hot Tin Roof. 223 S. UB 9039 – The Glass Menagerie. 149 S. UB 9178 – A Streetcar Named Desire. 199 S. UB 9240

Philipp Reclam jun. Stuttgart